ENCOUNTER
THROUGH THE
BIBLE

LUKE | JOHN

Copyright © Scripture Union 2011
First published 2011
ISBN 978 1 84427 578 6

Scripture Union England and Wales
207–209 Queensway, Bletchley, Milton Keynes MK2 2EB, UK
Email: info@scriptureunion.org.uk
Website: www.scriptureunion.org.uk

Scripture Union Australia
Locked Bag 2, Central Coast Business Centre, NSW 2252
Website: www.su.org.au

Scripture Union USA
PO Box 987, Valley Forge, PA 19482
Website: www.scriptureunion.org

The daily devotional notes for *Encounter through the Bible* have previously appeared in *Encounter with God*, a Scripture Union dated daily Bible guide.

The introductory material is adapted for this series from *The Bible in Outline* (Scripture Union, 1985) and *Explorer's Guide to the Bible* (John Grayston, Scripture Union, 2008).

British Library Cataloguing-in-Publication Data: a catalogue record of this book is available from the British Library.

Series Editor: 'Tricia Williams
Printed and bound in India by Nutech Print Services
Cover design by Heather Knight

Scripture Union is an international Christian charity working with churches in more than 130 countries, providing resources to bring the good news about Jesus to children, young people and families and to encourage them to develop spiritually through the Bible and prayer. As well as co-ordinating a network of volunteers, staff and associates who run holidays, church-based events and school groups, we produce a wide range of publications and support those who use our resources through training programmes.

CONTENTS

MEETING GOD

For many years Christians throughout the world have found the 'Scripture Union method' a tremendous help in deepening their relationship with God as they read the Bible. Here is a modern version of that method, which aims to help you to make your time with God a true meeting with him. You may like to refer to it each day as a supplement to the comments in this volume.

COME TO GOD as you are. Worship him for his power, greatness and majesty. Bring him your feelings and needs. Ask for his Holy Spirit to help you understand and respond to what you read.

READ the Bible passage slowly and thoughtfully, listening out for what God is saying to you.

TALK WITH GOD about what you have read. These suggestions may help you:

- 'Lord, thank you for your Word to me today. What special message are you shouting out to me, or whispering to me, in these verses?'

- 'Lord, I want to meet you here; tell me more about yourself, Father, Son and Holy Spirit, in these verses.'

- 'I don't know what today holds for me, Lord. I need your guidance, your advice. I need you to help me be alert. Direct my heart and thoughts to those words you know I need.'

- 'Lord, your Word is a mirror in which I often find myself. Show me myself here, as you see me, alone or with others. Thank you that you understand how I feel as I read your Word.'

- 'Lord, there are things here I don't understand. Please help me through the notes in this guide, or give me others who may help me.'

RESPOND Try to find a key thought or phrase which has come to you from this passage to carry with you through the day. Pray for people who are on your mind at the moment. Determine to share your experiences with others.

USING THIS GUIDE

Encounter through the Bible is a devotional Bible guide that can be used any time. It uses some of the best of the *Encounter with God* Bible series to guide the reader through whole Bible books in a systematic way. As *Encounter with God*, it is designed for thinking Christians who want to interpret and apply the Bible in a way that is relevant to the problems and issues of today's world.

It is hoped that eventually the series will lead readers through the whole Bible. This volume covers Luke and John. Look out for the other guides available now:

Old Testament
Genesis, Exodus, Leviticus
Numbers, Deuteronomy, Joshua
Judges, Ruth, 1 & 2 Samuel

New Testament
Matthew, Mark

The notes are arranged in Bible book order – in this volume, Luke and John. Each Bible book series begins with an introduction giving an overview of the book and its message. These aim to help you to get a grip on the book as a whole.

Each daily note begins with a call to worship which should help you consciously come into God's presence before you read the passage. The main 'explore' section aims to bring out the riches hidden in the text. The response section at the end of the note may include prayer or worship ideas and suggest ways of applying the message to daily living.

LUKE

Luke was a doctor and this is perhaps reflected in his concern for individuals. He was a friend and colleague of Paul and joined him on some of his mission travels (see use of 'we' in Acts 20,21; Colossians 4:14). His Gospel was probably written AD 62-70. This was the first of two volumes. In part 1 he wanted to write a well-organised account of the life of Jesus which was based on good eye-witness evidence (1:1-4). Acts is the second volume, which records the beginnings and development of Christianity.

Luke seems to write especially for Gentiles and to have a particular interest in children, women and social outcasts. He demonstrates throughout his Gospel that the good news about salvation, the good news about the kingdom and the good news as seen in Jesus is for all people, perhaps especially for the poor and powerless. He reminds his readers that Jesus is the fulfilment of this prophecy of the Messiah: 'The Spirit of the Lord is on me ... to proclaim good news to the poor' (Luke 4:18,19).

Outline

1 Introduction	1:1-4
2 The early days of the Saviour	1:5 - 4:13
3 The Saviour in Galilee	4:14 - 9:50
4 The Saviour goes to Jerusalem	9:51 - 19:44
5 The Saviour in Jerusalem	19:45 - 24:53

GOD WORKS OUT HIS PLAN

Lord, make me humble before you, to take the path you call me to, and to trust that your ways are best.

Luke opens his Gospel by telling us of his intentions (vs 1-4). Here, he says, is something solid, reliable, carefully investigated by going back to the beginning, and thorough. He wants us to read so as to come to an assurance and certainty about our relationship with God and have a solid basis for our faith (v 4).

Luke wants to tell us how God reaches out into humanity. He begins by showing how God's plan and the role played by John the Baptist are indicators of the detailed care God took to save us. He shows us, through Zechariah and Elizabeth, how he works through ordinary people, even when their response is marked by doubt as well as devotion. Elizabeth's plight of childlessness would have brought disgrace in those times (v 25). Yet despite her personal disappointment, she faithfully serves God (v 6, no doubt taking her disappointment to him), and when her situation is changed, she doesn't forget God but rejoices in what he has done. Zechariah also teaches us about walking with God, even amid uncertainty. He rather underestimates God and responds unbelievingly to his voice. It seems he needed a lesson in faith in the midst of his puzzlement.

Zechariah needed to learn that God will perform what he has promised, but in his time and his ways - which may be unexpected, even mysterious. The child to be born would play a vital role in God's purposes, and God's plan was worked out through the void in this couple's life being filled. Even the apparent random falling of the lot to Zechariah (v 9) was actually designed by God[1] not only to bring joy to this couple but also to fulfil the Old Testament promise that God would send someone to prepare Israel for a divine visitation.[2]

Why is it sometimes hard to trust the Lord, and believe that his ways for us are gracious and satisfying?

[1] Compare Ruth 2:3 [2] Mal 3:1; 4:5,6

THE GOD OF THE IMPOSSIBLE

Blessed is the one who believes that the Lord will do what he says.[1]

LUKE 1:26–56

What do you think are the really important points in these 31 verses? What do you think are the key things to notice about Mary? Sometimes popular piety has surrounded her in a haze of unreality, and she has been portrayed in ways that have little to do with the biblical text. It is clear that Jesus was conceived in her womb before sexual relations had taken place. Some people struggle to believe this, but if verse 37 is true, then we can accept it. Note how the angel explains the event: the Holy Spirit will come upon her, meaning that she will be enabled to do and be more than anything she could by herself. Then she is told that 'the power of the Most High' will overshadow her (v 35). If we want to see God work, we must listen for him to reveal how he does it.

Observe also how Mary responds to what she is being told. She is going to give birth to the Messiah, the one who God had promised would reign for ever, not just over Israel but over the whole world. This King would be God's Son. And Mary's reaction? 'May it be to me according to your word' (v 38). If God has promised something, he will always do what he says (v 45). Mary is available and willing to serve - basic characteristics that anyone can offer God. Mary will go where God leads, knowing that his grace will supply whatever she lacks. Mary's hymn is a story not only about herself but about anyone who fears the Lord and is the object of his mercy and favour, as verses 50–53 in particular emphasise. When God acts, the proper response is worship and praise, belief and trust, as well as obedience.

How do we respond when God is at work among us? Are we prepared for him to act as he wants? Do we believe he will keep his word?

[1] Compare v 45

TRUSTING GOD MORE

'Trust in the Lord with all your heart, and do not rely on your own insight'.[1]

Many of us are privileged to have been brought up in the ways of God and have benefitted from the godly influence of Christlike people. Unfortunately, this can sometimes have the effect of making us rest on our spiritual laurels. We may be steeped in the ways of the Lord, people of lifelong faith, but we still need to grow and build our relationship with God. Zechariah is such a person, a mature and pious man who still needed to learn. Sometimes God may have to deal with us if we have become complacent, and bring us up short and teach us of our need to keep moving forward in our service and knowledge of him.

Zechariah had, in effect, been brought up short by the Lord, and through his enforced silence been made to reflect and reconsider God's ways of working. God wanted to teach him that his sovereign will must be done, and while he sometimes works in surprising ways, trusting him is really the only path to take. Zechariah was learning that God brings his promise to pass in his own timing and in his own way, and he shows he has learned this by his obedience when it comes to naming his new baby (v 63). He demonstrates that even if those around him, his friends and neighbours, don't understand why he doesn't do things in the way they have normally been done (v 61), Zechariah will walk where God tells him to walk. And as he obeys, he is filled with joy and praises God for the way he has taught him.

'John' means 'God is gracious' or 'God has shown favour'. Today's verses show how God can use anyone who trusts him and wants to obey him and to know him better.

Ask the Lord to help you to reflect on where you are in your walk with him, and whether you need to grow in trust and obedience in any area.

[1] Prov 3:5, NRSV

GOD ACTS AT LAST

'Taste and see that the Lord is good; blessed are those who take refuge in him.'[1]

LUKE 1:67–80

Do you ever long for God to act, to relieve some pain and problems that you are going through, to bring refreshment in the midst of stress and strain? In these verses, Zechariah comes across as someone who has considered the painful trials and expectations of the past, and now, as he looks at his new baby, his lips are filled with rejoicing that God, at last, is going to do what he promised many, many years ago. Pain and sorrow had been the lot of his countrymen over many years, but people like Zechariah had prayed and trusted for a long time. They knew that God had made a covenant with Abraham (v 73),[2] as well as promising to send a Messiah and a prophet to prepare the way.[3] They had longed for these things to happen, and now they were all to come true.

How does Zechariah's song strike you as you read it? Some have interpreted it as a statement of how God is going to rescue his people, not least politically. Others see it in a more directly spiritual way, showing how salvation is being brought not merely to Israel but to the whole world. We should probably avoid polarising such views, and not make such a 'sacred/secular' divide. That said, it seems there is a greater emphasis on God's mercy (v 78), the forgiveness of sins (v 77), peace (v 79) and rescue from death itself (v 71), all coming about through the strong arm of God (vs 68,69). These points give a wider understanding of salvation, and show God coming to deal with the real problems of life in an all-embracing way. This is fulfilment of the promises of the Old Testament (note how full this song is of Old Testament phrases).

What areas of your life do you want God to act in? Take these to him and trust in his promises to meet your needs.

---

[1] Ps 34:8 [2] *See* Gen 22:15–18 [3] Isa 9:6,7; 11:1,2; Mal 3:1; 4:5,6

THE CREATOR AS A BABY

'Our God contracted to a span, / Incomprehensibly made man.'[1] Bow in adoration!

LUKE 2:1–7

As you read these seven verses, what strikes you? What hits me is the simple, humble origins of Jesus' birth. It can be hard to appreciate who it is that is born here: the 'King of Kings and Lord of Lords'.[2] Most royal figures are born with great rejoicing and ceremony, but this birth is as lowly as it comes. Being placed in an animal's feeding trough, spending his first hours of human existence in a manger, is to enter this world in about as mundane a way as possible. If I was arranging the birth of the Saviour of the world, I would have organised a rather more spectacular entry!

Perhaps one of the things we see here is that God's ways are so often different to ours. The arrival of the incarnate Son of God provides a contrast between how God did it, and how we might have done it. In Luke 1, we saw how the angel said the baby would be a king of an everlasting kingdom (vs 32,33), and Zechariah rejoiced that he would be like the rising sun who gives light to guide us in the way of peace (vs 78,79). Yet this birth is so plain. The self-emptying of the Messiah, taking the form of a servant, has begun.[3] Maybe we shouldn't stop at the manger, though; the birth of this baby is the start of the confrontation between the kingdom of God, in all its seeming insignificance and vulnerability, and the kingdoms of this world. This, not the Emperor Augustus, is the true King. He probably never heard of Jesus; but within a century or so, his Roman successors were trying to wipe out Jesus' followers. And 200 years after that, the Emperor himself became a Christian!

Take time to wonder at the ways of God, his faithfulness and humility, the way he brings about his plans, and his love for the human race.

---

[1] Charles Wesley, 1707–88, from 'Let earth and heaven combine' [2] Rev 19:16
[3] Phil 2:5–11

GOD USES UNLIKELY PEOPLE

Lord, help me to understand how you use people to do your will and make your ways clear to others.

LUKE 2:8–20

God often works in surprising ways and with people who seem unlikely candidates to do his will. Why do you think God chose the shepherds to be among the first to receive news about the Saviour and Messiah? Some think this indicates how God meets with the outcasts and unpopular, but that is not how shepherds would have been viewed at that time. The way shepherds appear in Scripture is usually positive, and their association with these events is more likely to indicate God's involvement not just with the prominent and great but with all people.

Further, what the angels announced to the shepherds that night is proclaimed to all humanity. As the shepherds tell everyone what has happened (v 17), and people are astonished at what they say (v 18), we sense anew that God does what he promises and involves all sorts of people in spreading his good news.

How amazing that God involves himself with us! Let us not take this for granted. Let's make sure we take time to ponder and really see who and what Jesus is all about. The praise from the armies of heaven reflects the wonder of who he is - not merely one teacher or leader among many, but the Saviour who is Christ the Lord (v 11), one who is now seated at the right hand of God, praying for us.[1] No wonder Mary kept these things in her heart, treasuring them and thinking about them often (v 19; *cf* v 51). Yet God had only just begun to reveal the way he is involved with us through Jesus. This Saviour was sent from heaven to die for us, be raised for us, and to relate to us! This is the true story of Jesus - no wonder the shepherds glorify and praise God.

Lift up your voice in praise and offer yourself in gratitude for what this birth means!

---

[1] Luke 22:69; Heb 7:25

ALWAYS HOPE IN GOD

Lord, help me to see how doing the ordinary things of life is important in your sight.

LUKE 2:21–32

Sometimes our regular, daily lives can seem rather ordinary and mundane. Yet one thing these verses tell us is that we should carry out whatever role God has given us, however plain it may appear to be. The key thing is to be faithful and committed to the Lord, desiring to serve him in whatever way he wishes. Mary and Joseph have a trusting attitude of worship and obedience in taking Jesus to be circumcised and presenting him to be dedicated to the Lord. This was their responsibility as parents. Simeon illustrates how one can live a life carefully following God in an unspectacular way and serving him with an attitude of joy and submission.

This can lead us to consider how we represent Jesus in all that we do. To appreciate and see him is to love the salvation he brings, to perceive his light, to see him as the Word of God.[1] Jesus was a servant, and calls us to walk in his footsteps. Our testimony to him, the way we live our lives and speak of him, should give others a chance to see Jesus. Thus in Matthew 25:40,44,45, for example, Jesus says that when we serve those in need, we are serving him. Simeon had served God faithfully and consistently – he seems to identify with doing God's will and to trust in his timing. He is a servant who wants to do only what God tells him. His reward for such service is to see the one long awaited, who will bring salvation to all peoples (vs 26,30-32). He knows he can be contented with his life, as he has now experienced what the Lord has promised.

Ask God to make you a vessel in his service, content with doing whatever he asks, looking to serve him and make him known, however he sees fit.

[1] John 1:1

GETTING PRIORITIES RIGHT

How can I maintain right priorities when life is throwing hardships at me?

LUKE 2:33–40

Most Jews in the first century believed that a great champion would soon come to earth to revive the old glories. Since they were God's chosen people, he would surely intervene and rescue them in their plight of living under foreign occupation. There were a few Jews, however, who didn't dwell on thoughts of power and armies. They were known as 'the Quiet in the Land', and they devoted themselves to a life of constant prayer and quiet, patient watchfulness, waiting till God should act. Simeon and Anna were two such people. They had trusted the Lord throughout their lives, and were now in the situation of seeing God answer their prayers.

Simeon's words here must have brought sober reflection to Mary and others who heard them. The Promised One of Israel will lead to the falling as well as the rising of many in the nation.[1] Some will oppose him (v 34), and their reaction to him will reveal how they respond to God. For Mary, the words of verse 35 are challenging. She will experience pain when she realises that 'the claim of Jesus' heavenly Father outranks any human attachments between him and his mother',[2] as she will start to see in tomorrow's verses. When she sees his priorities, what will be her priorities?

Anna was an old lady, a widow, who had never ceased to hope, and had given her life to prayer and worship. Life may well have been difficult for her, but her faith had grown deeper as she sought God's priorities for her. Both she and Simeon were nearing the end of their lives, but both were at peace. They had walked with God and served him, and now had the honour of witnessing God's salvation.

When life is challenging, we can rebel against God or trust him as our Father. How do the three people in today's verses encourage us to do the latter?

---

[1] See Isa 8:14,15; 28:13–16 [2] R Brown, *The Birth of the Messiah*, Doubleday, 1993, p465

UNDER JESUS' AUTHORITY

Do I see Jesus as the unique Son, whose attitude, claims and priorities are my model?

LUKE 2:41–52

Why do you think Luke has included this story? Perhaps the key is in verse 49, where Jesus underlines his unique call as well as his unique relationship to God. As soon as we try to evaluate him, we realise he transcends any normal human categories. He is one who not only makes amazing claims but also does things that are surprising and unexpected.

Here we have Jesus staying behind in Jerusalem and his parents at first assuming he was with the rest of the group. When they find him he has been missing for three days, and they discover him among the teachers in the Temple, asking questions and responding. Jesus amazes his listeners with his deep understanding of the things of God.[1] Mary makes plain their frustration, which has left them with great anxiety (v 48), the word referring to deep anguish.[2]

Jesus' reply is blunt and to the point (v 49). His priority, even at this early stage, is to do God's will, to be involved with divine issues in the Temple, the place of teaching and worship. He is already being driven by his intimate, personal relationship with God.[3] He had to do his Father's work, this idea being a favourite of Luke when he shows how God's plan is being fulfilled.[4]

Jesus' attitude to his call to serve God and his relationship with his Father reveals in him an authority that transcends basic human relationships and makes Mary's indirect rebuke almost irrelevant. Yet he is a picture of how we should all prioritise our lives before God, sometimes having to make choices that may be hard for some to understand, as we seek God's face and pursue his ways.

Lord, help me to meet Jesus again and, through him, to know God more closely as I seek to learn his ways and follow his example.

---

[1] *See* Luke 8:56 for a similar reaction   [2] *See* Luke 16:24,25 for a similar use of the word   [3] Luke 10:21,22   [4] Luke 9:22; 13:33; 17:25; 24:7,26,44

NO SHADES OF GREY

'Look deep into my heart, God, and find out everything I'm thinking. Don't let me follow evil ways, but lead me in the way that time has proved true.'[1]

LUKE 3:1–20

John bursts on to the scene preaching an uncompromising message of repentance. It received a mixed reaction. Proving highly unpalatable to some, as the concluding scene demonstrates, the crowds nonetheless flocked to him to receive a tongue lashing for their sinfulness and complacent reliance on their Abrahamic heritage. John's coming reinstated the role of prophet in a setting where many devout Jews feared that God would not speak to his people again. Luke stresses that John's announcement of the coming Messiah is rooted in a time and place where, behind the list of names and locations, lay a story of oppression and misery that had been building up to boiling point.[2]

It was common practice for the road to be improved before a king made a long journey, and John was doing what Isaiah had foretold[3] in preparing a highway of people's recognition of their need of a saviour, one more powerful than John who would bring judgement as well as mercy (vs 16,17). This was to be no tame Messiah. Moreover, the message was for all humanity not just the Jews (v 6), pointing to Luke's particular concern for Gentiles. Vital though they were, repentance, forgiveness and baptism were not enough. John issued a stark challenge to his listeners to provide authentic evidence of personal change. In contrast to the usual diet of strict religious observance required by the rabbis, he stressed instead the need for lives of simplicity, generosity, honesty and integrity. Against a backdrop of injustice and oppression, people who received baptism were committing themselves to be those in whom God's justice could be seen. Receiving the good news should result in living the good news (v 18), and John's challenge echoes down through the centuries to us today!

How might God make your life a highway for him to come to those you'll be with this week?

[1] Ps 139:23,24, CEV [2] Tom Wright, *Luke for Everyone*, SPCK, 2004 [3] Isa 40:3–5

KNOWING OUR ROOTS

'Yet to all who did receive him, to those who believed in his name, he gave the right to become children of God.'[1] By God's grace, that is your identity.

LUKE 3:21–38

In an uncertain world, knowing where we come from can be important. This is illustrated by the popularity of TV programmes in which famous people trace their ancestry and by the growth in internet genealogy research. This passage is about who Jesus is, with implications for both him and us. At the start of Jesus' ministry, Luke reminds us of his divine identity and his human roots. He is God's Son and the final one of a list of sons traced back to Adam. In giving us this family tree, stretching back to creation, Luke is telling us not just that Jesus is Israel's 'Messiah', another meaning of 'son of God', but that all creation would benefit from what he came to do.[2] The genealogy in Matthew's Gospel[3] differs significantly in places: it is much the same from Abraham to David, but diverges from that point on. One explanation for the difference is that in a small nation like Israel it's possible to trace one's ancestry through different routes.

Jesus is baptised, although it's not necessary, and in so doing identifies himself fully with us in our sinfulness. As he's praying, heaven opens, his Father speaks, and a dove (an early Christian symbol of the Holy Spirit) descends upon him. Picture the scene; dwell on the warm, rich and full affirmation given by his heavenly Father. What a wonderful statement! Yet it's one that echoes the Old Testament in pointing to the Messianic Servant figure who must follow the path of suffering for the salvation of many.[4]

Jesus knew who he was and what he had come to do. In him heaven and earth came together – eternity contracted into a human frame, into a man who at the age of 30 embarked on a journey that led ultimately to a cross.

How does knowing that you are a loved child of God affect your engagement with others and your view of your family background?

[1] John 1:12 [2] Wright, *Luke* [3] Matt 1:1–17 [4] Isa 42:1

THE JESUS WAY

'Jesus. Jesus. Jesus. Jesus is the way we come to God. Jesus is the way God comes to us.'[1] Give thanks to God for Jesus.

LUKE 4:1–13

'A glorious beginning. A great start. The baptism, the descent of the dove-Spirit, the voice from heaven. Yes. Momentum is up. Jesus is on his way. And we who are ready to follow Jesus are also on his way.'[2] Surely this can't be right? Having announced their campaign, what an effective public leader does is to keep building their profile, getting out there and engaging with the public. Already we see that Jesus doesn't fit the mould, that the way he goes about leadership is profoundly countercultural. What in fact happens is that Jesus, full of the Holy Spirit, is led by that same Spirit into the wilderness, where he is tempted by the devil for 40 days. He apparently goes willingly, and Mark tells us that he goes 'at once',[3] with no hanging around for autographs!

Time in the wilderness grappling with the temptations was essential if Jesus was to be fully prepared for the task ahead, also modelling for us the 'how' of authentic discipleship. The temptations clarified at the outset the ways in which he would do his work as the Messiah, what living in the kingdom of God[4] would look like. Paul too spent time in the wilderness after his conversion,[5] indicating that seasons of testing and temptation are purposeful and shouldn't be feared or run from.

We may know we are God's children and be reasonably sure of his calling on our lives, but the key question is how we go about living those lives. The devil didn't try to get Jesus to renounce his identity or his call. Rather, he focused on the ways in which Jesus would pursue it, on what it meant for him not just to be the way to God but also the way of God for us to emulate.[6]

Study the temptations. Then pray for courage to live the Jesus way, the way of the kingdom.

---

[1] Eugene Peterson, *The Jesus Way*, Hodder & Stoughton, 2007 [2] Peterson, *Jesus* [3] Mark 1:12 [4] Luke 4:43; Matt 3:2 [5] Gal 1:17 [6] John 14:6

RIGHT NOW

'But encourage one another daily, as long as it is called "Today".'[1] Thank God for those who have encouraged you in your faith over the years.

LUKE 4:14-21

Jesus' fame had been spreading, and when he went home to Galilee he did so differently, in a vital way, from the boy they had known growing up. He returned 'in the power of the Spirit' (v 14). And audaciously he claimed that he was impelled and equipped by that same Spirit to be the fulfilment of Messianic Scriptures,[2] verses about blessing rather than judgement. Three times in the Greek text in verse 18 the pronoun 'me' is used in an emphatic position.

He read a Jubilee text,[3] widely applying the themes of good news to those who are poor, needing healing, or freedom from debt and captivity. The gospel of God was for all people, including those on the margins and even those outside Israel. For example, the Greek word for 'release', used in Leviticus to describe what happens in the Jubilee Year, occurs here twice.[4] This was no mere ethical code or system of beliefs. Jesus was ushering in a new era of salvation in the fullest sense. It was here now. And he was to be the means of it happening. For the listeners that was a remarkable claim, and we will soon look at their reactions.

For us this is the heart of the gospel, good news upon which we are to base our lives as Christians. In this the 'today' word (v 21) is important. Jesus' contemporaries didn't doubt that God's kingdom would come some day, but they probably weren't expecting God to be at work in their midst just then. Jesus' teaching was different, though, in that he saw God acting in the present.[5] How about you? Are you familiar with the words but don't expect the immediacy of 'today'? Think again. Isn't the sheer scope of what Jesus promised breathtaking, something to get excited about, and risk taking hold of once more?

Prayerfully reflect on Jesus' announcement. How might that apply in a workplace setting and what could you do about it?

[1] Heb 3:13 [2] Isa 61:1,2; 58:6 [3] Lev 25 [4] Simon Jones, *Discovering Luke's Gospel*, CBG; Crossway Books, 1999 [5] Leon Morris, *Luke*, IVP, 1974

PLEASING PEOPLE

'For in him we live and move and have our being.'[1] Praise God for the all-encompassing nature of our relationship with him.

LUKE 4:22–30

You'd think that as Jesus was setting out on his public ministry he would go out of his way to keep on side the people most likely to support him, namely those from his home town. Not at all. Although they are initially impressed by the manner and content of his synagogue speech, his popularity was very short-lived. It was almost as if he went out of his way to shake them up with his focus on the Gentiles, to startle them out of their complacent view of the privileges accompanying their status as God's people. His message shocked them deeply because of their desperation for God to liberate Israel from Roman occupation. Several Jewish texts of the time expressed longing that God would annihilate these pagans,[2] so Jesus' inflammatory reminder to them about the main beneficiaries when the prophets were active being Gentiles not Jews did not go down well.[3] He certainly wasn't interested in getting the vote of the people of Nazareth!

Nonetheless, winning popularity can have a powerful pull. Viewing figures for programmes like *Britain's Got Talent* indicate that a significant proportion of the public in some way identifies with the contestants' hunger for recognition. However, given the speed with which many then fade into obscurity, it's obvious that popularity can be a fickle friend. Think too about the pressure on politicians to please people: if they don't they're unlikely to be re-elected. Being liked by others can make us personally feel good, too, so, it's all too easy to speak and act on the basis of how it will affect people's opinion of us. Jesus loved people but he wasn't a 'people pleaser'. Confident of his Father's love, what mattered to Jesus far more than being popular was the bigger picture of what God was doing in the world and his part in it.

Pray for politicians to maintain integrity and make good and wise decisions not merely based on winning popularity.

[1] Acts 17:28 [2] Wright, *Luke* [3] 1 Kings 17:7–24; 2 Kings 5:1–14

WORDS AND ACTIONS

Reflect on the ways God has shown compassion towards you over the past year, and give him thanks for his never-failing love.

LUKE 4:31–44

These verses are packed with activity. Having controversially announced his mission in his home synagogue, Jesus starts implementing it in Capernaum, Simon's town, where he finds a much warmer welcome. Imagine the sounds, the smells, the crowds jostling to get help or a better view, and the sheer drama of it all. Voices calling for attention, demons shouting out his name, groups huddled together speculating about the source of his authority. There's a sense of momentum but his quiet authority over demons and sickness speaks volumes.

His kingdom manifesto comes vividly to life as we find him with those on the margins (people demonised or sick; and women), focusing on their individual circumstances and not merely offering sympathy but bringing transformation. His words and actions come together, with one validating the other.[1] He moves purposefully from one situation to the next – from the synagogue to a family home to a solitary place,[2] and then on to other towns. There's urgency in his preaching about the 'kingdom of God' (v 43) – the first use of a phrase that is found over 30 times in Luke's Gospel.[3] And he demonstrates a clear sense of what he's come to do, having been sent,[4] and so refusing to be diverted, however pressing the immediate circumstances (vs 33,34).

As I write, horrific pictures of disaster in Haiti are filling the TV screens, but by the time you read this something else will have taken its place. Whatever the situation, it's easy for our senses to become dulled, to feel distanced from the needs of others. Yet Jesus started his mission right in the midst of human need, always purposeful, always loving.

Decide to listen to news programmes regularly. Adopt the practice of praying about what you hear, asking Jesus to show you how to respond.

---

[1] Jones, *Discovering* [2] *Cf* Mark 1:35 [3] *NIV Study Bible*, Hodder & Stoughton, 1987 [4] Luke 9:48; 10:16; John 17:18

AMATEUR FISHING!

Meditate on the 'incomparable riches of his grace, expressed in his kindness to us in Christ Jesus.'[1]

LUKE 5:1–11

This passage provides an intriguing insight into the early influences on Simon Peter's faith, the man who went on to be such a significant leader in the early church. This wasn't the first time that he and his fishing partners, James and John, had been with Jesus. On this occasion Jesus uses what appears to be a merely practical course of action, launching out in a boat to have sufficient space to address the crowds, as an opportunity to demonstrate his authority and power.

Through a deeply unsettling (vs 8-10) series of events he showed Simon, and those with him, that there was no separation between religious life and common workplace practices, that he is Lord of all. Jesus moved seamlessly from speaking 'the word of God' (v 1) to giving instructions to experienced fishermen about how to do their job. He took hold of their everyday experience and transformed it. Fish are more likely to be caught in the dark, and following an unsuccessful night's fishing it must have seemed ridiculous to follow Jesus' instructions. However, the phrase that Simon uses, 'But because you say so, I will...' (v 5), is one that rings down through the centuries to encourage and challenge us in our normal workday settings. When Jesus is present, something new and unexpected can be brought out of failure – but for that to happen we need to cooperate with him.

From that moment on, Simon Peter's life would never be the same. The experienced fisherman learnt what it was to come under the all-embracing authority of Jesus and what it meant to be led by someone greater than him. He who went on to lead the early church learnt at the outset that 'Biblical leadership always means a process of being-led';[2] no area of life falls outside this.

Encourage your church to create space for discussion and prayer about workplace issues. How could you support a work colleague going through a tough time?

[1] Eph 2:7 [2] Martin Buber, *Israel and the World: Essays in a Time of Crisis*, Shocken, 1963

TRANSFORMING TOUCH

'May the God of hope fill you with all joy and peace as you trust in him, so that you may overflow with hope by the power of the Holy Spirit.'[1]

LUKE 5:12–16

Our earliest, most life-affirming experiences involve touch. To be touched by someone motivated by love, kindness or compassion can be healing. It says we are present to them, have worth, and that we somehow belong. Children who haven't been hugged much or whose main experience of being touched has been harmful often end up psychologically damaged and unable to sustain healthy adult relationships. At the other end of the age spectrum an achingly sad dimension of older people's isolation in Western societies can be the absence of human touch.

It's particularly noteworthy that Jesus here broke strong religious and social taboos and deliberately 'reached out his hand and touched' (v 13) a man with an advanced case of 'leprosy' (a name given to various skin diseases in biblical times). In its worst form, this disease was disfiguring and fatal, and was so dreaded that the only defence was quarantine.[2] To come into physical contact was to break the purity laws, so to prevent this happening accidentally sufferers had to call out 'unclean' whenever other people were around.[3] This must have been a deeply humiliating experience.

For this man, Jesus must have seemed his last hope. Dependent on others because he had no way of earning a living, yet shunned and unlikely to have been touched for many years by anyone free of disease, he would have heard the stories about Jesus' healings but wasn't sure that Jesus would really look at him. Most of us don't doubt that God can heal. Rather, our struggles are with whether he will. There are no easy answers, but this incident demonstrates how Jesus' deep compassion translated into immediate action. Healed and with instructions for reintegration into society,[4] this man experienced at first hand God's passion for those on the margins.

Who are the 'untouchables' for you? What attitudes to others do you need to repent of and do something about?

[1] Rom 15:13 [2] Leon Morris, *Luke* [3] Lev 13:45,46 [4] Lev 14

GRACE AND TRUTH

'How much more will those who receive God's abundant provision of grace and of the gift of righteousness reign in life through the one man, Jesus Christ!'[1] Prayerfully reflect.

LUKE 5:17–26

This is the first time that Luke mentions the Pharisees. They are out in force to observe Jesus at work, along with other religious leaders from every village across the region (v 17). Why such large numbers? Maybe because they saw the coming kingdom of God as their exclusive concern and so were checking out this upstart young preacher with his outrageous claims.[2] Their name means 'separated ones', and there were about 6,000 of them spread across Palestine.[3] They were teachers in the synagogues, religious examples in the eyes of the people, and self-appointed guardians of the Law. They believed that if only people would fully observe the Torah this would create the conditions for God to act and liberate his people from pagan oppression. As it was their job to promote this, they were hardly likely to be a sympathetic audience.

Luke contrasts their sceptical judgemental attitudes with the faith of the men who were so desperate to get help for their paralysed friend that they broke in through the roof. With all eyes on him, Jesus speaks the 'blasphemy' of forgiveness of sins. He repeats the word 'forgive', stressing it as the central issue.[4] To everyone's amazement, a miraculous healing takes place.

It's easy to criticise the Pharisees, but most were trying to do the right thing although in the wrong way. They were so sure of themselves that they failed to spot God himself! They saw themselves as protectors of the truth, zealous for God's righteousness, but their slavish pursuit of the Law left little room for grace or generosity. Today, in our relativistic society, it is easy to be so concerned with defending the truth, holding the moral ground, that we forget to be gracious people. May we, like Jesus, be 'full of grace and truth'.[5]

Maintaining a balance between grace and truth is hard. Which side do you err on? Ask the Holy Spirit to show you where you need to change.

[1] Rom 5:17 [2] Wright, *Luke* [3] Jones, *Discovering Luke's Gospel* [4] NIV Study Bible [5] John 1:14

PARTY TIME!

'He brought me to the banqueting house, and his banner over me was love.'[1] Praise God for his extravagant hospitality towards you today and every day.

LUKE 5:27–39

Probably the main thing Peckham people would miss if our church didn't exist would be our community parties! I think this is a good thing, born from a conviction that parties can be a sign of the kingdom if they deliberately include those on the outside, those considered unacceptable by others. Today's story once again powerfully demonstrates Jesus' focus on people on the margins, with parties as a key element. In Jesus' day tax officials were extortionists, Roman collaborators, regarded highly suspiciously and as ritually unclean by the Pharisees – but Jesus chose to break into their world, just as he did into that of the man with leprosy, by summoning Levi to follow him.[2]

Jesus redrew the boundaries about who was in and who was out.[3] He didn't merely call people like tax collectors to follow him but he also sat down to meals with them (v 29). Eating together was a sign of acceptance, and the Pharisees had strict rules about table fellowship as an indication of who were true Israelites. Jesus, however, rewrote their criteria, putting recognition of need and repentance at the heart of the matter. When they used John the Baptist as an example of religious austerity, Jesus again highlighted the party theme, a wedding feast, as a sign that a new age had come, with celebration central to this. He wasn't saying that fasting was a bad thing,[4] but that the need was over for the type of fasting in Judaism that was a lament that God's kingdom had not yet come.

Meals feature a lot in Luke's Gospel as a radical sign of the kingdom,[5] yet in today's church we've mostly reduced this to invitations to people like ourselves or hospitality rotas. Maybe we should have fewer meetings and more parties!

Prayerfully consider how your mealtimes could become a 'kingdom sign' for those who don't yet know Jesus.

1 Song 2:4, AV 2 Wright, *Luke* 3 Jones, *Discovering* 4 *See* Matt 4:2; 6:16–18
5 Luke 7:36; 9:12–17; 10:38–42; 11:37; 14:1; 19:7; 22:14; 24:30,41–43

SHRIVELLED HEARTS

'The sacrifices of God are a broken spirit; a broken and a contrite heart, O God, thou wilt not despise.'[1]

LUKE 6:1–11

Jesus often has a run-in with the authorities. Their rigid interpretation of the Law seems oppressive and nit-picking, a tool for finding fault rather than a way of glorifying God. Jesus does not respond to their rebuke to his disciples defensively. He argues with them on their own terms – showing that even with their own reference points, they have got it wrong. His answer produces no change in their attitude, indicating that there is some other motive behind their words; their real aim is not to protect the Sabbath but to attack Jesus. That is why, when Jesus produces the amazing miracle in the synagogue and heals a man with a shrivelled hand, they completely miss the significance. Instead of seeing the glory of God in the power and compassion of Jesus, they see their own power becoming diminished and their authority challenged.

If this were an example of simple jealousy we might understand it. Many people are jealous when they are upstaged by another, or when someone gets the acclaim they would like. If we're spiritually awake, we notice when this happens in our own lives, and ask God to help us to be more secure in who we are. But the Pharisees don't do that. They allow their attitudes to harden. The chief emotion that drives them is not jealousy but hatred. Each time they attempt to undermine Jesus, the hatred grows deeper, because he exposes their hypocrisy and misuse of power.

This story challenges us all. Whenever legalism replaces faith, our spiritual lives wither. We become afraid to admit what we get wrong, and don't ask for God's grace and forgiveness. Like the Pharisees, we can be blind to miracles, and miss the power and love of God. Yet Jesus can still heal, and not just shrivelled hands, but shrivelled hearts also.

Lord, we bring our motives and desires to you and ask that you challenge and change us and keep us from hardness of heart.

[1] Ps 51:17, AV

BLESSINGS AND WARNINGS

'Do not fear, for I have redeemed you; I have called you by name, you are mine.'[1]

LUKE 6:12–26

It is not clear what criteria Jesus used for calling 12 apostles out from his larger group of disciples. From the list of names, it doesn't seem to have been related to any special qualities. Levi, for example, wasn't among them, even though he was generous and totally committed.[2] Judas Iscariot was, even though he was mean-spirited and untrustworthy.[3] What is clear is that Jesus spent the night in prayer before he made this big decision. It is a sober reminder to us of how much more we need God's guidance in the decisions we make.

The ministry of the twelve seems to have started very quickly. It must have been startling to see Jesus with the crowds, bringing healing. Even more startling was his teaching, not least these 'beatitudes' and 'woes'. Here in Luke, they are more terse and shorter than in Matthew's Gospel, and relate less to attitudes than to the basic conditions of life. But the effect in both Gospels is the same. Jesus turns normal values upside down. Far from bringing defeat or curse, poverty, hunger, weeping and rejection can bring blessings. It is the things we welcome – riches, food, laughter and good reputation – which can go sour and bring misery.

What is the difference between those Jesus calls 'blessed' and those he warns with 'woe'? The 'blessed' seem to be those who have put their trust in God despite the circumstances they face, even when it brings persecution. The 'woes' have put their trust in material well-being, seeking joy in riches, good food and flattery and living self-centred lifestyles. It is an apt description of cultural values today. Indifference to the hungry or broken-hearted is always the wrong way for those called to follow Jesus. His warnings of the consequences are not just for Judas and the disciples, but for us also.

What would be the greatest happiness you would wish for yourself? And what do you fear most?

[1] Isa 43:1, NRSV [2] Luke 5:27–30; some, of course, equate Levi with Matthew [3] John 12:4–6

LOVING AT ITS HARDEST

If there is someone who has behaved like an enemy towards you, think of them now, and read this passage with their name on your mind.

LUKE 6:27–36

This passage marks the dividing line between Christianity and every other way of life – we're to love our enemies. This injunction makes no sense at all in the world's eyes. What Jesus is urging is not just non-retaliation, where we don't hit back or go for vengeance. He's asking us to make ourselves utterly vulnerable to someone who hates us or treats us as an enemy. There can surely be nothing more risky than responding to evil with love.

But we shouldn't misunderstand the motive behind these actions. It is not so that an abuser can violate us further. Jesus isn't giving permission for someone to act unjustly or cruelly. He's rather urging us to live out the maxim of treating others the way we would like to be treated ourselves (v 31), and this is far from foolish. If I behave badly towards someone else, it is an enormous relief to discover that she is not going to hold it against me or try to get her own back. When she doesn't recite my wrongs, nurse the injury, tell everyone what a terrible person I am, but 'turns the other cheek', she relates to me in a way that holds back her woundedness and gives me space to reflect. It diffuses my anger. It helps me to face what I have done. It increases the likelihood that I will see my guilt, and experience the pain of remorse.

None of this makes loving our enemies easy. Supposing the enemy doesn't repent? Supposing evil triumphs and our offer of love is abused? What then? The answer is that then we begin to understand just how radical is Christ's love for us, and how demanding is the way of the cross. We also realise that we have to leave the final outcome to God.

'Love is patient, love is kind ... it is not easily angered, it keeps no record of wrongs.'[1] Let us ask God for more of this love.

[1] 1 Cor 13:4,5

SETTING STANDARDS

'Surely you desire truth in the inner parts; you teach me wisdom in the inmost place.'[1]

LUKE 6:37–42

We often think that we will be judged according to God's standards for our lives. So it comes as a surprise when Jesus tells us we will be judged by our own standards. Whatever judgements we make about other people will be applied to us. If we criticise others, the same criticisms will be held against us. If we show generosity to others, we will receive an abundance in return.

This teaching warns us against hypocrisy. We can't impose standards on other people that we don't live by ourselves. But it is also a warning against self-delusion. Very often we don't recognise hypocrisy in ourselves. The story of the mote and beam makes this point so well. The image is such an exaggerated one – how could anyone notice a speck of sawdust in someone else's eye if he had a great plank obscuring his own vision? And how on earth could he be so unaware of the plank? Yet we are so often unaware of our own faults and failings; all too ready to point out those of other people.

Churches have split because of the way people judge others rather than themselves, and the same tendency damages marriages, families and neighbourhoods. It spoils work and ruins international relations, and even causes wars. Yet, as Jesus shows us, it is ridiculous. The first step out of hypocrisy is simply to live by the standards we impose on everyone else. For then we will begin to realise how wrong they often are, and have the humility to seek a better way. That better way is very reassuring. It involves generosity of spirit; giving rather than criticising, warmth rather than judgement. The picture Jesus paints is of a measure that is packed full and overflowing with kindness (v 38), reflecting God's own generosity which heals and replenishes and never tears down.

Let us ask God to remove what obscures our vision, and to safeguard us against self-delusion.

1 Ps 51:6, NIV 1984

MY HEART IN MY MOUTH

Think of the people whom you always like to be with. What is it about their characters that you most enjoy?

LUKE 6:43–49

Visiting a hospital ward, I used to sit at the bedside of a frail old lady who had few visitors. She had outlived her generation. As I got to know her she talked about many things and many people. Almost everything she said was charitable, gentle and kind. She was a wonderful illustration of verse 45; there was so much goodness and gratitude stored up in her heart that it overflowed into almost every conversation. The fruit of her long life was sweet and good. It was a joy to share it and realise how many others she had blessed.

Jesus reminds us here that we show the state of our heart through what comes out of our mouths. Our spiritual condition becomes evident in the fruit we bear. And, however much we might try to disguise it, this is more obvious to other people than we realise. The kind of people we are deep down will sooner or later be evident to everyone in our journey through life. Jesus' story about the two builders reinforces the point. If we have no depth, it will be obvious, for any storm will leave us exposed and devastated. We need deep and strong foundations, a firm base to build upon. Just as only good trees bear good fruit, and good hearts produce kind words, only good foundations make strong buildings. Everything else produces decay and will not withstand destruction.

How do we begin to put down good foundations or store good things in our hearts? It requires self-examination, prayer and repentance. We need to ask God to show us what we are like. We also need, as in verse 47, to come to Christ to hear his words and be committed to putting them into practice in our lives.

'Search me, God, and know my heart; test me and know my anxious thoughts. See if there is any offensive way in me, and lead me in the way everlasting.'[1]

---

[1] Ps 139:23,24

SURPRISED BY FAITH

'Thou art coming to a King, Large petitions with thee bring; For his grace and power are such, None can ever ask too much.'[1]

LUKE 7:1–10

This incident contains many surprises, but at its heart is an expression of faith that surprises even Jesus – this is the only time that we read of him being amazed. The centurion is marked by many admirable characteristics – his regard for his servant, his love for the Jewish people, his humility – but the one that marks him out is the nature and measure of his faith. We cannot miss the fact that Jesus comments especially on the surprise of this faith being found outside Israel – faith can be found in places we would not always look and it is wise not to put up artificial barriers where God has none. The Spirit moves where he chooses,[2] and works throughout the world.

The centurion's faith is born out of his understanding of authority. Knowing what it is to stand in a line of command where instructions are to be carried out to the letter, he understands, as perhaps others do not, the authority of Jesus. Presumably his faith is based on some experience; perhaps he had developed his knowledge of Israel's God through building a synagogue. Certainly he knew something of Jesus. Faith must be based on an understanding of Jesus' authority if it is to have any meaning. Are our prayers based on the vague conviction that God, acting in and through Jesus, might be able to do something, or are they based on the conviction that we are coming to the King of the universe who has ultimate authority over all things? This is not to say that we will always get what we ask, for God has authority over us too, but it is to say that we can afford to come and make our requests in the total conviction that he has the power to act.

Where have you seen faith that surprised you? How did you react? What will you learn from it?

---

[1] John Newton, 1725–1807, 'Come, my soul, thy suit prepare' [2] John 3:8

AMAZED BY LIFE

'But mayest thou, thyself, O God of life, Be at my breast, be at my back; Thou to me as a star, thou to me as a guide...'[1]

LUKE 7:11–17

Familiarity dulls us to the further surprises in this incident. We know that Jesus raised people from death, so we are used to the idea – but for them this is full of shock. Life was short, funerals frequent, and women not always highly regarded, so it is surprising that an itinerant rabbi would be deeply moved by the sorrow of one woman (v 13, the Greek implies a degree of entering into her pain). It is quite unthinkable that he should touch the bier, since this would cause him to become ritually unclean and any good Jew would do anything to avoid this – including crossing the road.[2] But an even bigger shock awaits, as Jesus commands the corpse to get up (v 14).

God and God alone could give life. The great prophets of the Old Testament, Elijah and Elisha, had been used in this way,[3] but apart from that the only precedent is creation. So by this action Jesus is setting out his stall in a clear and dynamic way. At the very least he appears as a unique servant of God, endued with an authority not seen for centuries. The reaction of the crowd is therefore not surprising – and the verb translated 'come to help' is used in the Greek version of the Old Testament of God coming to save.[4] Jesus has come to inaugurate the new era of God's reign, when death will be conquered. This young man would die again, but Jesus would later rise with a new quality of life, the first of many.

The danger is that we tame Jesus, robbing him of his break with convention and his demonstration of the presence of the kingdom through acts of power. Far from shocking, he is now held up as a model of conformity rather than as the creator and giver of life who brings the transforming power of God into the world.

Take time to thank God for the new life he gives us in Jesus and for the assurance of the resurrection.

---

[1] K Jones, *Songs of the Isles, Selections from Carmina Gaelica*, Canterbury Press, 2004 [2] Luke 10:31,32 [3] *See also* Luke 4:25–27 [4] Exod 3:17; 4:31 in the LXX

DISTURBED BY DOUBT

'My soul is downcast within me; therefore I will remember you.'[1]

LUKE 7:18-35

In contrast to the centurion who exercises unprecedented faith and the woman who experiences the power of God without the exercise of faith, John faces doubt. Luke gives us another indication of Jesus' Messianic identity, and in doing so he gives us a model for handling our questions.

Doubts are part of the life of faith. John the Baptist, who earlier had demonstrated clear understanding,[2] is in prison, as Luke has already informed his readers.[3] As so often in our own experience, circumstances and the failure of God to act in the way that he expected have left John wondering what is going on. Too often, our doubts are suppressed as wrong, incompatible with faith, a sign of weakness. Once after confessing to doubts I was thanked by someone, saying that for 15 years she had assumed that she was the only one. This should not be: it is better to take our questions, as John does, to the place where we can find help. Jesus points him to the evidence of his actions, and relates them to the promises of the Old Testament.[4] This involves a reorientation: John had been expecting a different sort of Messiah and he now has to think of the 'compassionate Benefactor of the poor',[5] rather than the conquering King and Judge. We, too, find that our doubts can lead to a reorientation in which we now see things not from our perspective but from God's. This can be painful, as it was for John, but there is no way forward while we cling to our own false securities based on incorrect understanding. The life of faith requires facing up to doubt and moving through it to a new place of faith. Without this, we end up like many of Jesus' contemporaries - responding neither to the prophetic challenge of John nor to Jesus' invitation to enter the joy of salvation (vs 31-34). Only with God's wisdom can we perceive the truth.

How does your church respond to those who have doubts and questions? How might you give them greater support?

1 Ps 42:6 2 Luke 3:1–22; John 1:29–36 3 Luke 3:20 4 Isa 29:18; 35:5–10; 61:1
5 Joel Green, *The Gospel of Luke*, NICNT; Eerdmans, 1997

OVERWHELMED BY LOVE

'For you know the grace of our Lord Jesus Christ, that though he was rich, yet for your sake he became poor, so that you through his poverty might become rich.'[1]

LUKE 7:36–50

Building on the contrasts of the previous stories, here we have another sharp contrast – between the self-righteous Pharisee (v 39) and the devoted and forgiven 'sinner' (v 47), almost certainly a euphemism for prostitute. It also adds to our growing understanding of the real nature of Messiah, who has come to save broken sinners, not to confirm the religious and political prejudices of the religious elite, and who is not afraid of disturbing the status quo and (again) shocking the establishment in the process. Jesus' approach to confrontation is interesting. His story draws Simon in, forcing him to commit and therefore reassess his own position. The more subtle, oblique approach of story may work where direct confrontation does not.

Simon is sure of his place in society, he is acceptable, he conforms to the Law. The woman, too, knows her place as an outcast whose immorality means that she has no place among the people of God. And yet she has found acceptance; her actions can only be explained if she has had some previous meeting with Jesus. Where do we stand? With the reckless, emotional abandon which recognises the immensity of what God has done for us in Christ or the formal right-living of Simon? We know the answer we would like to give – but how does the evidence stack up? When did we last engage in an action which looks remotely like that of this woman? And if we find that hard, can we really claim to have understood the nature of sin, grace and forgiveness?

Grace always surprises, always disturbs; it cannot be forced into our ways of thinking. The Pharisees had no real answer to sin, except to condemn it; Jesus goes to its root. In doing so he makes, as we have seen before,[2] a clear claim to be acting with God's unique authority.

It is the church's mission to announce this grace with openness, generosity and love. How do we match up?

[1] 2 Cor 8:9 [2] Luke 5:24

DIVIDED BY RESPONSE

'Open our eyes, Lord, we want to see Jesus ... Open our ears, Lord, and help us to listen.'[1]

The parable of the sower is sandwiched between the note about the women who supported Jesus, and who by implication are included among the circle of disciples, another staggering break with convention, and that about his family who, it appears, were not fully supportive.[2] The whole sequence challenges us to review our response. Jesus is looking for attentive listening (v 18) and practical obedience (v 21), resulting in action which can be seen by all (vs 16,17). The women illustrate the point. Their actions may be costly – perhaps more significant than the financial cost would have been the sly glances and raised eyebrows. There is still a cost to following Jesus, but it is too easy to be less than fully committed.

Luke has already introduced a contrast between those who hear and those who respond. The parable illustrates this, but it also suggests that understanding is not always as easy as we pretend. In contrast to the usual assumption, Jesus speaks in parables not to make understanding easy but to ensure that listeners must give careful attention to find the significance. Following him is a demanding business, which starts with teasing out the nature of his call on our lives. It continues with the hard business of living out the truth in the face of many alternative attractions or demands, the power of which has not diminished over the centuries. Put in the effort, however, and we shall discover the principle of growth: understanding is rewarded with greater understanding. At first reading verse 18 may seem harsh, but this is not about ability, nor does it discriminate against those whose understanding is limited; it is about motivation and priorities. So the key message for us here is this: what occupies our time and attention, and how does it reflect the message of Jesus?

Pray for any you know who are finding it hard to hear and understand what Jesus is saying.

1 Robert Cull © 1976 Maranatha Music/Adm by CopyCare 2 Mark 3:21; John 7:5

AMAZED BY POWER

'To you, O Lord, I lift up my soul. O my God, in you I trust.'[1]

LUKE 8:22–25

Luke continues to move towards the climax that we shall reach in the next chapter – the disclosure of Jesus' identity. Each of the stories we have looked at raises the question in some way and hints at the answer. For us, reading from a post-Easter perspective, the answer is obvious, but for Jesus' contemporaries he was something of an enigma. Our perception may not be as accurate as we think, however; our understanding of Jesus is shaped by 2,000 years of history and is formed against the background of our own culture. If only we could struggle with the disciples in their boat we might find something fresh.

His exercise of power and authority startles them – and would startle us were we not so familiar with the story. The nature of their question is not simply occasioned by the exercise of raw power but by the parallels with the creation story, where the Spirit of God hovers over the chaotic waters and brings order. For those who will see, Jesus is demonstrating again his unique nature and his divine authority. He has power over the natural elements, the preserve of the Creator God.[2]

We may sympathise with the disciples. In the light of their incomplete, but growing, awareness, is it not hard of Jesus to rebuke them for their lack of faith? Maybe, but they had plenty of evidence and were often slow to see the significance.[3] We have more evidence, but is our faith any stronger? Confronted with the struggles and uncertainties of life, where do we turn? Too often the answer will be that we turn to our own skills and experience or to the experts of our age rather than recognising that we have with us the Creator of the Universe. We are, after all, the products of our rationalistic age. Faith is not always the easy or the obvious option and may well go against the grain.

Pray for a faith which can see beyond the immediate to the power of God at work in his world.

[1] Ps 25:1,2, NRSV [2] See also Ps 65:7; 89:9; 107:29 [3] Mark 8:14–21

FREED BY AUTHORITY

'You're all I want in heaven! You're all I want on earth!'[1]

This account presents several challenges. We cannot be entirely certain where the event takes place, but it is in Gentile territory. We worry about the pigs, forgetting that Jesus' priorities may not have been ours and that the ancient world viewed things differently. We find the demonology primitive, forgetting that Jesus was communicating in the context of his time and that our own understanding of the demonic has been overly influenced by centuries of scientific rationalism.

Jesus' authority is demonstrated again, this time over the demonic powers. Throughout Jesus' life a spiritual battle rages. The kingdom of God is breaking in and powers are being challenged. Sometimes, as here, the demons express an understanding of Jesus and his ministry and a recognition of his power which goes beyond that of the disciples or the onlookers.[2] They know that their days are numbered. Once the demons have been dismissed (and possibly in the minds of the onlookers destroyed, for some believed that demons were destroyed by water), and the man cured (Greek 'saved'), we observe again differing reactions. How do they, and we, respond to Jesus? The man wishes to follow, his compatriots want to be rid of Jesus. The man has a task to perform – to tell what God has done. Luke subtly makes the point that he went and told what Jesus had done. The full revelation of Jesus' person is yet to come but Luke cannot resist hints. It is not clear why Jesus sometimes invites following, sometimes commands silence and sometimes requires the story to be told. In our situation we have to determine our response. What do we make of Jesus? What is the story we shall tell? Is it one of powerful deliverance from, and victory over, the powers, whatever form they take in our world, or do we secretly wish that Jesus did not disturb the status quo quite so much?

Identify some stories that you could tell to help your friends understand more about Jesus and his ministry.

1 Ps 73:25, *The Message* 2 Mark 1:34; Luke 4:34,41

HEALED BY TRUST

Come to God today, recognising your weakness and inviting him to work in those aspects of your life where you feel special need.

LUKE 8:40–56

Power marks Jesus' ministry; it comes from God,[1] brings healing[2] and is available through the Spirit to his followers.[3] Here we see that power exercised over sickness and we also learn that when Jesus heals his power is expended. This reminds us of his humanity and warns us that ministry for us too, even when exercised in the power of the Spirit, will mean sacrifice and weariness.

The idea of faith is particularly prominent in this section of Luke, bringing healing and forgiveness. We cannot know what the level of this woman's understanding was, but she had enough knowledge to believe that Jesus could make a difference and to show great faith. Her intervention must have distressed Jairus, apparently robbed of hope by her intervention, but her faith and its result may well have been an encouragement to him at the moment of crisis (v 50, where 'believe' has the same Greek root as 'faith'). The link between faith and healing is a complex one, perhaps the more so because we make distinctions which would not have been quite so clear in the New Testament – the word for 'cured' here, as so often, is the same as the word for 'saved'. Luke wants us to see Jesus as the Saviour of the world. Salvation is the key issue – physical healing may or may not be part of it, and when it is it demonstrates the presence of the Saviour, drawing our attention to the larger picture. Whether we are thinking of salvation or physical healing, it is faith which brings the power of God to bear. Without it, even Jesus is limited in what he can do,[4] and yet he sometimes heals where no faith is present. While it is unreasonable and untrue to suggest that individuals are not healed because they lack faith, the New Testament encourages us to have more faith so that we might see more of God at work.

How is your faith is expressed in practice? What more might you experience if you had a deeper conviction that God is at work in the world and in us?

[1] Luke 4:18,19; 5:17 [2] Luke 6:19 [3] Luke 24:45–49; Acts 1:8; *see also* John 20:21,22 [4] Matt 13:58; Mark 6:4–6

LEARNING BY PRACTICE

'Holy, holy, holy is the LORD Almighty; the whole earth is full of his glory.'[1]

LUKE 9:1–9

In the ministry of Jesus, the presence of the kingdom demanded demonstration as well as proclamation; it was to be the same for his followers. Jesus' training was typical of his time: the disciples gathered around the teacher or rabbi, learning on the job through discussion, listening, observation and practice. The demonstration consists of both works of power and a simple lifestyle of faith and dependence on God. The responsibility to preach the good news still rests with the church,[2] but the extent to which the model of these verses is to inform our practice is less clear. Some of the instructions seem to be specific, and the Christian community after Pentecost operates in a variety of ways which show both similarities and dissimilarities.

There are, however, principles which transcend any particular time or situation. The disciples are given power (that which Jesus expended in healing the woman) and authority (that which the centurion recognised in Jesus). Both are present in the ministry of the church.[3] We announce and demonstrate that the rule of God goes beyond Easter and Pentecost. We may differ on exactly how this will happen in practice today and we have to live with the paradox that power is often shown in weakness – but words, important though they are, are never enough. There is no way to undertake mission except in dependence on God.[4] Our calling is to announce through word and action that the rule of God in Christ has begun and to call people to allegiance to him. For us, as for these first 'missionaries', there is an urgency to the task; time is not to be wasted. We are to travel light, showing what it means to be a pilgrim people focused on another realm,[5] and we are to preach for a response.

Pray for the members of your church in their daily mission in the world – at home, at work, at leisure.

---

[1] Isa 6:3 [2] Matt 28:18–20; Acts 1:8 [3] Acts 4:33; Rom 15:19; Matt 28:18–20; 2 Cor 10:8 [4] 2 Cor 12:9,10 [5] Phil 3:20; Heb 11:13–16

BLESSED BY PROVISION

'The eyes of all look to you, and you give them their food at the proper time. You open your hand and satisfy the desires of every living thing.'[1]

LUKE 9:10–17

It seems that a debrief with the disciples was interrupted. Luke uses the term apostle for the twelve, but only now are they discovering what it means to be sent. Despite all they have seen and experienced of Jesus they still have much to learn. Faced with the need of the crowd, their first reaction is to make it someone else's problem (v 12), a reaction which we may find all too common in our own experience. When Jesus throws it back to them their sense of confusion and inadequacy is all too evident; the chances are that we have found ourselves in similar situations. There is nothing to do but offer Jesus the meagre resources available and see what he will do with them.

What happens evokes varied responses. It is another demonstration of the power of Jesus, an expression of compassion, and a suggestion that meeting practical needs is part and parcel of the good news – but it goes beyond that. To those present it inevitably calls to mind the only previous individual to feed the masses. Here is a prophet like Moses,[2] a figure who had come to be part of the messianic vision of Judaism. Jesus is again laying claim to be the Messiah, the One through whom the provision of God for the people is being made available, and as Luke records this incident he is again looking forward to the significant moment which is about to occur. At a yet deeper level, the act of giving thanks and breaking the bread, which demonstrates the presence of God in all of life and is normal for any devout Jew, will in the minds of the later reader recall two other incidents in the Gospel.[3] We are invited to see Jesus, crucified and risen, as the answer to the needs of the world.

As we look out on a world of need, what are we doing to help people find satisfaction in Jesus? How are we demonstrating his ability to provide for every eventuality?

[1] Ps 145:15,16 [2] Deut 18:15,18 [3] Luke 22:19; 24:30

CHALLENGED BY SACRIFICE

Pause to reflect on the wonder of God come to us in human flesh. Give him praise and thanks for his grace and love in humbling himself in this way.

LUKE 9:18–27

We have arrived; the moment to which Luke has been building has come. This is the hinge on which his Gospel turns. Shortly[1] he will start his account of the journey to Jerusalem, which occupies a large part of the Gospel, but first comes the recognition that Jesus is indeed the Messiah. Readers have seen this since 4:18, but the disciples have struggled with the concept as he did not fit the expected mould. However, Peter, and no doubt the others too (for it is unlikely that they would not have discussed this among themselves), have come to this point of certainty. True, their understanding is still far from complete, but that should not detract from the significance of this moment.

No sooner is the truth recognised than further shocks await. Jesus' messianic destiny is death (unthinkable) and resurrection (incomprehensible). Worse, before they have had a chance to take this on board, they are told that their destiny as his followers is death also. As followers of Jesus we have to recognise that death is the way to redemption. If that was startling in their world it is no less and perhaps even more startling in ours. Life is everything, success is all, power is the way forward – and the gospel of the kingdom undermines and subverts these values and shows a different way, one of self-sacrifice. Are we being shaped by this gospel or by the values it has swept away? Too often as followers of Jesus we look little different, too readily we buy into the power and self-interest of this world rather than the weakness and self-sacrifice of the kingdom.

For some of our brothers and sisters the threat of physical death is real and ever-present; for others a profession of faith will mean loss of reputation or job prospects. Perhaps the time to be concerned is when opposition has no practical effect whatsoever on our lives.

Pray about the way in which you live your life, asking God to show you ways in which you could follow the example of Jesus more closely.

[1] Luke 9:51

LUKE

OVERCOME BY GLORY

'Yours is the day, O Lord, and yours is the night; let Christ, the Sun of Righteousness, abide in our hearts always.'[1]

LUKE 9:28–36

As if to counter the effects of the announcement of impending death, Jesus gives his closest followers a glimpse of the other side of the picture. Jesus' much-debated statement about those present not dying before the kingdom comes (v 27) is best seen as a reference to the inauguration of the kingdom through his own death. Death and glory are impenetrably interlinked. For John the hour of Jesus' death is the hour of his glory.[2] Even here amid the glory there is a reminder of death. As Jesus meets with Moses and Elijah, representatives of the Law and the prophets but also figures with strong Messianic overtones, they discuss his departure. The word is exodus. At one level it means way out or departure, but especially in the presence of Moses it evokes memories of God's great saving actions in the past and sees Jesus' death in similar terms. The paradox is poignant; the glorious Son, the One whom the Father loves[3] is chosen – for death, and through death the salvation of the world. Here on a mountain, in a cloud bringing to mind the giving of the Law, grace comes to the fore. The writer of Hebrews expands on this picture.[4]

It is hardly surprising that the disciples are confused and overcome. Nor that Peter hasn't a clue how to respond. Do we, with the benefit of hindsight, do any better? We tend to emphasise either the power and the glory or the weakness and sacrifice, each to the detriment of the other, but the life of Jesus contains both, and so do our lives as his followers. We can hold our heads high as those who serve the King of Glory, as followers of the chosen Son, chosen ourselves in him, but we are called to serve others, just he did.[5] Even as we rejoice in our glorious calling, we live for others and must be prepared to die for them.

In what ways has your view of Jesus been challenged over the last few days? How will this affect the way you live for him?

[1] *Celebrating Common Prayer*, Continuum, 1992 [2] John 12:23 [3] Luke 3:22
[4] Heb 12:18–24 [5] Mark 10:43–45; John 13:14–17

UNDONE BY AMBITION

'Lord, I do not have much to give – but such as I have I offer to you, to be inspired by your love, touched with your compassion and empowered by your Spirit.'

LUKE 9:37–50

It is easy to understand the sense of frustration which Jesus feels at the slowness of the disciples[1] – but we stand in the disciples' shoes rather than Jesus'. We think we have our theology sorted, we are moved by the power of worship, and then we are confronted by human need that we cannot meet. Jesus attributes this failure to a lack of faith. As we have seen, it is too simplistic to assume that if we had more faith everything would happen as we desire, but we still have to face the challenge: if only we really believed might we see more of God's power at work? Matthew adds Jesus' saying about faith as small as a mustard seed.[2] Mark makes it clear that prayer is also involved.[3] Service demands a high level of commitment.

After such an abject experience of failure and with the rebuke of Jesus still ringing in their ears, it seems amazing that the disciples should be fighting over pecking order. A moment's reflection, however, will tell us that this rings true to human experience. It may be worth taking time to reflect on our own desire for status and placing ourselves in the position of the child (v 47), remembering that it is to the unassuming that the kingdom is given.[4] To those who have little self-image, Jesus issues the invitation to a higher seat;[5] to those who have too high an estimation of themselves he offers the model of the child.

The same model warns us against exclusivism (vs 49,50). We naturally put up barriers and keep out those uncomfortable people who do not see or do things the way that we do, but Jesus would have us honour whatever is done in his name, in line with his mission and character.

Are there those of whom you are aware who struggle to experience acceptance within the church? Pray for them today. Look for ways of showing the love of Jesus.

[1] Mark 6:52; 8:12; John 14:9 [2] Matt 17:20 [3] Mark 9:28,29 [4] Luke 18:17 [5] Luke 14:7–11

NEW PRIORITIES

Lord, help us to follow you without looking down our nose at strangers or looking back to our friends and family.

LUKE 9:51–62

Today's passage is all about family and tribal concerns. In the individualistic West, it is difficult for us to see how radical Jesus' teaching is. The obligation of a son to bury his father was an important part of honouring one's parents. Similarly, saying goodbye to your family doesn't seem unreasonable. After all, the man must be serious about leaving them for Jesus or he wouldn't be saying goodbye. There is a close parallel with Elijah's calling of his disciple Elisha, who was out ploughing a field. Elisha also asked to say goodbye to his people. Though Elijah said yes (albeit reluctantly),[1] Jesus' demands are greater and he allows no compromise as regards loyalty.

Earlier in this chapter we were told that 'people' thought of Jesus in terms of the prophets,[2] but the readers and the twelve know that he is even more important than that. We are dealing with the Messiah, one who effects change, rather than with a prophet who talks about change to those in power. That's why they think it's time for fireworks in the first part of the passage (vs 54,55). John the Baptist had looked for the one who was to come, who would baptise with fire and judgement.[3] That is what Jesus will do, but not now.

What we learn from Jesus through this passage is that his work begins a new era. He is not just a leading prophet within the old system of priorities, rather his presence signals a whole new set of priorities. He teaches that there is a new age, with new demands. It is not yet the time for enacting judgement, but, as we shall see in the passages that follow, our actions in this new era are connected to what will happen at the judgement.[4]

Make a list of five people you dislike and five whom you love. How can you best submit these relationships to God?

---

[1] 1 Kings 19:19–21 [2] Luke 9:18,19 [3] Luke 3:16,17 [4] Luke 10:13–15

MERCY AND JUDGEMENT

Lord, help me to offer good news and mercy.

LUKE 10:1–16

This is déjà vu for at least some of the disciples. At the beginning of chapter 9, before Peter's confession, Jesus had sent out the twelve with very similar orders. Perhaps this is different; in this sending we are explicitly told that the disciples were not going to these places in Jesus' stead, but they go to places Jesus was about to visit personally (v 1). Was their purpose, therefore, to identify hospitable places where Jesus could indeed visit (vs 8,9) and inhospitable places which would not then receive a visit from their Lord (vs 10-12,16)? The people's attitude will not change the fact, however, that in Jesus, 'the kingdom of God has come near' (vs 9,11).

Our circumstances of mission are different and, even for the disciples, details of the instructions here will be rescinded[1] - but perhaps there is some lesson for us. There is a difference between what is recommended here and what the disciples tried to do in yesterday's passage - to call down the fire of judgement on an inhospitable village.[2] Here, they are told to wipe the dust from their feet (v 11) as a testimony against inhospitable people,[3] and this will result in, and is a sign of, coming judgement (v 12). The significant difference, of course, is between inflicting judgement and announcing judgement in the spirit of warning. The difference is clearly visible in Jonah's ministry in Nineveh.[4] Our job is to concentrate on the message and on the mercy offered, not, as Jonah did,[5] on the judgement reserved for the unrepentant. Even as we shake the dust off our feet, we should be saying to those with whom we disagree that 'the kingdom of God has come near' (v 11).

Return to yesterday's list. Think of concrete ways to bring good news to those whom you don't particularly like. What might 'shaking dust from your feet' look like in your context?

---

[1] Luke 22:35,36 [2] Luke 9:54 [3] Luke 9:5 [4] Jonah 3:4,10 [5] Jonah 4:2

WE CAN MAKE HIM SMILE

Thank you, Lord Jesus, that just as you share the Father's joy so we can share your joy as we concentrate on pleasing you by doing your will.

LUKE 10:17–24

What a delight! This is one of the most encouraging passages in the New Testament. Over the years, we have all got used to stories in the Gospels that display the disciples' lack of understanding and their inability to see what is in front of their noses. We have all studied passages where Jesus asks them, 'Where is your faith?' or rebukes them.[1]

But here, when the 72 come back to him, it is with joy (v 17). And his reaction? Jesus too is full of joy (v 21). How wonderful. Maybe you are like me – I so often feel I'm letting him down. Even when I'm doing what I think he wants, my efforts seem so small and the results so meagre. As we shall see later in this series, when we feel that way, we should not try to justify ourselves. His joy and love for us are based on his mercy, not on our excuses. This passage shows us that his standards for us are not so impossibly high. Our obedient submission can be enough to make him glad, as he sees the fulfilling of the Father's will through us.

Here is one more thing I love about this passage. I am used to people saying, 'I'll pray for you' when things are going badly. But here are the disciples returning to Jesus with joy – things have gone well – and what does Jesus do? He talks with them, first; he does not neglect that. He also shares their joy, as we have seen: he rejoices with those who rejoice.[2] But then he quickly turns to pray to the Father. Perhaps we too should practise bringing God into our joys as well as our problems.

When someone tells you about something that's going right (not wrong!), pray for them. Prepare to tell them about Jesus' example in this passage when they look confused!

---

[1] *See* Luke 9:55 [2] Rom 12:15

ATTITUDE BEFORE ACTION

Pray that God would give you the attitude of dedication rather than calculation.

LUKE 10:25–37

You know the story so well. Today, let's look at the man to whom the story is told. He's very like you and me. We're past the stage of wanting to test Jesus (v 25), though we may also have started there. Rather, we're likely to be with the man at the stage of justifying ourselves (v 29).

Maybe you're like me. Sometimes I speak simply to say things. Other times I seem to speak to position myself: 'I think so, too, boss,' or 'Well, not everybody feels the way that you do.' I know when I'm speaking this way; I can feel myself looking around the room afterwards: 'Ah, but is that really worship?' 'Ah, but what is truth?'[1] 'Ah, but who is my neighbour?' (v 29). Perhaps you've been trapped in this attitude when Christmas draws near. Your address book is bulging and you think, 'Who must I send a card to this year and who can I get away with leaving out?' The man in the story is responding to Jesus' challenge to love his neighbour by asking how few he can love and still technically fulfil the brief.

The Christian life is full of characteristics that you don't acquire by seeking. You don't get more humble by trying to. You don't become more loving by trying to. You don't become generous by trying to. Focus on yourself – on your characteristics – and you'll fail. 'Whoever tries to keep their life will lose it; and whoever loses their life will preserve it.'[2] You become these things by focusing elsewhere – on others, on Jesus. Yes, the difference between the man and the Samaritan is action, but the action arises from an attitude: not 'I don't want to serve more than my fair share; who must I serve?' but 'Anyone need anything?'

Think of three people who you could help, whether it might be expected or not, whether they deserve it or not. Then give them what they need.

---

[1] John 18:38 [2] Luke 17:33

ATTITUDE OVER ACTIVITY

Pray that God will give you the quietness of heart to be attracted to him, rather than being distracted and busy.

LUKE 10:38–42

Just as Jesus shocked those around him in yesterday's passage by suggesting that one of the hated tribe of Samaritans could be more faithful than the most Jewish of Jews,[1] so in this story he will shock people by accepting a female pupil, a truly unheard-of and disturbing act in his culture.

Now look at something else. The man to whom Jesus told yesterday's parable sought limits on his service. Martha, in today's passage, does not. She is serving like mad. Yet it is not she but her sister who is commended. Why? In part it is probably because of her implicit criticism in verse 40. And Jesus never seems to respond very well to the words, 'Don't you care?'[2] But her outburst is typical of servants whose focus is still on themselves. Martha seems less concerned at the effect Mary's idleness will have on the guests and more on the effect it has on Martha: her sister had left her to do the work by herself. 'Tell her to help me' (v 40). Mary's contribution is minimal, but her attitude is right. She's focused on Jesus.

'Only one thing is needed,' says Jesus (v 42, NIV), which reminds us of the story of the rich young ruler. 'You still lack one thing,' Jesus said to him, continuing with what sounds to us like two or three things: 'Sell everything you have and give to the poor ... Then come, follow me.'[3] But it's not three things, it's one. The one thing needed is the one thing Mary chose: to focus on Jesus. True service follows from that. It is never a substitute for that. Sure, a faith that is not accompanied by action is dead,[4] but works that distract (v 40) from faith are not what is called for either! Like Mary, choose Jesus and follow through on the implications of this choice.

Look at your list of three people from yesterday. Pray about these people, using a listening prayer.

---

[1] Luke 10:31–33 [2] Cf Mark 4:38 [3] Luke 18:22 [4] James 2:17

HOW DISCIPLES PRAY

Trust in his love. Pray for boldness and confidence.

LUKE 11:1–13

Jesus gives a three-part answer to the disciples' question about how they should pray. He gives them a form of words that they can use, and he then goes on to give them clues about the attitude with which they should pray.

The prayer Jesus gives has some suggestive points of contact with John's preaching[1] and with ancient Jewish prayers, but what I find most interesting are the juxtapositions. God is holy, the one whose very name is to be hallowed, and yet he is Father. Our sins are forgiven, even as we are working out the pattern of forgiving in our own lives. The Lord's prayer, or, as it's sometimes called, the disciples' prayer, is deceptively simple, full of riches in its overtones and harmonies. Matthew gives us more of it,[2] but in Luke, Jesus moves directly on to more teaching about prayer.

The story of the friend at midnight initially shocks the reader, with its implication that God helps you because of your boldness or audacity rather than because of his relationship with you! To understand, we need to go to verse 13. If you, being fallible and human, know how to give what is good, then how much more will God know how to give the best gifts? The argument is from the lesser to the greater, and that is how we should understand the story of the friend at midnight: if your 'friend' who was unwilling to help out of friendship can be motivated to help because of your boldness, then how much more should boldness work on God, whose friendship and loving kindness never fail?[3] The message of the first story is to pray with boldness. The message of the second, however, is to pray with confidence. Verses 9 and 10 are the hinge that summarises the two.

Recall the people you prayed a listening prayer for yesterday. Pray with boldness and confidence about something you heard then.

---

[1] Luke 3:7–14; *cf* 5:33 [2] Matt 6:9–13 [3] Luke 18:1–7

HEALTHY OR VACANT?

Lord, help me to concentrate not only on what you have freed me from but also on what you have freed me to.

LUKE 11:14–28

This is a complex passage, with difficult twists. It is made even more difficult for us moderns by unfamiliar supernatural subject matter. But at its core, the passage is not meant to teach us about demons as such. Rather this is a story about the purpose of Jesus' ministry. Let me explain. There are various reactions to the exorcism of the man, but Jesus did not want people to see this as an end in itself. By itself, an exorcism is only an invitation for a new infestation (vs 24-26). Instead, there must be an invitation to bring something better into your life.

Now the demon is the strong man guarding his residence, and Jesus is the stronger man who divides up the plunder with his gang. His strength, his success, should prove to you that he is working with God's power (v 20) and that you should join 'his gang', There is no neutral (v 23). Even the person who has been delivered from a demon is not necessarily permanently free, only vacant. Ironically, those who objected that it was by being in league with demons that Jesus did what he did and asked for a sign (vs 15-16) were closer to the truth than the woman who thought his mother was blessed (v 27). She was marvelling as if the event was the goal. They at least knew that the events and wonders were signs and pointers to the nature of Jesus and his work.[1]

So what should we do? Let us go beyond being thankful for our deliverance as if that were an end in itself, as if he has neutralised sin and freed us to be normal, empty and ready for eight more demons. Let us go on to be with him, be alongside him and filled with him.

Pray that God would fill you with his Word and his Spirit to help you hear and obey.

---

[1] *Cf* John 6:26,27

THE LAMP OF THE BODY

'Lord, spit on our eyes that we might see.'[1]

We again find this confusing language from Jesus. The subject matter and the analogies, which must have been plain to Jesus' initial hearers, are a lot less familiar and straightforward for us. I found the lamp-eye-light passage especially difficult because of its apparent similarity to the more famous passage in Matthew's Gospel,[2] but in Matthew Jesus' followers are the light of the world for others to see. Our passage is more about how people should see and react to Jesus.

One greater than Solomon is here, one greater than Jonah is here, and there are clear signs of it. The lamp-eye language is thus another version of 'Whoever has ears to hear, let them hear,'[3] but using the analogy of eyes and light rather than ears and sound. The people of Nineveh saw Jonah and repented. The people of Jesus' age should also repent – they can see the one who is greater than Jonah, provided they have not hidden themselves away or stuck their head in a bowl or have eyes that are unhealthy.

This is teaching aimed at the crowds rather than the disciples (v 29), and it is instructive and perhaps comforting to us when we have such trouble getting our friends or family to see just how wonderful and amazing the Lord Jesus is. It should be no surprise to us if they cannot see what is before their faces. If Jesus' contemporaries refused to take proper account of him when he was in the flesh before them, well, perhaps it's understandable that people can be blind to him now. There's also a word for Christians here, however, particularly in the dark times. Let us be sure to keep our eyes fixed on Jesus[4] and not like a lamp that is hidden or under a bowl!

When are you tempted to shut your eyes to Jesus? How can you remind yourself to keep your eyes on him?

1 Bruce Cockburn, 'Broken Wheel' 2 Matt 5:14–16 3 Luke 8:8; 14:35
4 Heb 12:2

WHAT? ME TOO?

Lord, give me the grace to listen and change.

LUKE 11:37–54

Today's passage sometimes strikes us as uncharacteristic of Jesus. He should be nice and affirming to people, especially people with a rich spiritual tradition of their own, even if he does not share it. However, the Gospels have several incidents like this.[1] Could he have been fully human if he had never felt frustrated and angry?

For me, the fiercest bit comes in the middle, when the experts in the Law feel themselves unfairly lumped in with 'ordinary' Pharisees. They all concerned themselves with meticulous obedience, but the experts scoured the Scriptures to work out how to obey. From their tone, they expect Jesus to see them differently, as they do themselves (v 45). It sounds as though they agree with his criticisms, but find them too sweeping. Perhaps by criticising those who tithe without justice and mercy, they feel he condemns anyone who tithes, merciful or not. Perhaps by criticising those whose goals are the seats and greetings, they feel he is demeaning anyone who accepts such accolades, even when it's not their goal. Like the earlier expert in the Law,[2] they try to justify themselves. They feel they have grounds on which to do so. They expect an answer like: 'Ah, you are right. Apologies, my friends.' What they do not expect is for Jesus to turn around and direct equally venomous criticisms at them!

What should they have done? What should we do? When we feel ourselves implicated in Jesus' criticisms, our first thoughts should not be how to avoid criticism or make excuses. Too often, our goal is to change people's perception of our foibles rather than to change ourselves. We should allow criticism to bite. For there can be no doubt that few things are more characteristic of Jesus than this: he hates self-justification.

Think of a time recently when you have fended off criticism. Reconsider.

---

[1] Mark 3:5; Luke 20:45,46; John 2:15,16 [2] Luke 10:25–29

JESUS' FRIENDS – IN PUBLIC

What are you afraid of? What would be life's worst possible scenario? Lay down your fears at the Lord's feet, safe in the knowledge that he cares for you.

LUKE 12:1–12

This section begins with a remarkable picture. Surrounded by 'thousands' of people trampling on each other to get to Jesus – doubtless bringing their sick in droves – Jesus chooses to speak 'first' to his disciples. This is the premium he sets on equipping people for leadership in the kingdom of God!

For these potential kingdom leaders, Jesus has a remarkable message: make sure your fear is well placed! The Pharisees are 'hypocrites', because they fear public opinion. They are willing to say things in private they would be ashamed of, if published – which is precisely what will happen (vs 2,3)! How ready are we for that kind of transparency? Public opinion may want to crucify Jesus and his friends (v 4), but that's not the real thing to fear. Rather, we should fear God, who could do far worse things to us, if he wanted to (v 5). But praise him, his heart towards us is not for destruction, but for delight (vs 6,7). He even counts our hairs! A God who delights in us like that deserves 100 per cent loyalty from us – and he calls us to show that loyalty by acknowledging Jesus publicly, relying on the Holy Spirit to give us the words when called to public account (vs 8-12). Our standing in heaven depends on our readiness, now, to be public friends of Jesus Christ.

The sin of blasphemy against the Holy Spirit (v 10b) is not failure to acknowledge Jesus, but rather ascribing Jesus' power and influence to the devil. No followers of Jesus would ever do that – but how often do we just keep quiet about our Christian faith, preferring to merge into the crowd rather than be distinct? Here, Jesus' disciples are a distinct little circle, eagerly listening to his teaching while the crowd mills around them. Let's not be afraid to be identified with Jesus.

Offer up your fears to God in honesty, and pray for courage in your discipleship today.

THE MISERY OF MIDAS

Yesterday, fear; today, money. Often we use money to keep fear at bay. Examine your feelings about money, and thank God your Father that true security is found in him.

LUKE 12:13–21

Someone in the crowd manages to catch Jesus' attention, and we discover why at least one person has travelled to find him. He's suffered an injustice, and wants Jesus' authoritative intervention. Jesus' response is ironic (v 14) – of course, he has been appointed judge and arbiter, in fact of the whole world! He has just claimed this, in verses 8 and 9.[1] But he is not a judge who serves our interests, who can be pulled into our agenda. Rather, he is concerned to judge the underlying motives that draw up our agenda in the first place. Are we seeking to 'store up things for ourselves', or to be 'rich towards God' (v 21)?

The theme of God's judgement continues from verses 5 to 9. We will one day render account for the way we have used our wealth. Have we served ourselves with it, or used it for God's kingdom?[2] I work at London School of Theology, which was established largely through the benefaction of Sir John Laing, founder of Laing's construction company. Sir John was a deeply committed Christian as well as being extremely wealthy – but his estate at his death was valued at just a few hundred pounds, because by then he had given it all away. Today, the Laing family trusts are still supporting a multitude of kingdom causes as a result of his determination not to store up wealth for himself but to be rich towards God.

We need to ask radical questions of ourselves, both individually and corporately. The fact that we may not be as rich as Sir John Laing doesn't excuse us from his example. Do we use our money for the kingdom? And how will rich Western churches, and countries, answer the charge that we have failed to share our wealth with the poor of the world?

Turn this passage into prayer. Is God calling you to use your money for the kingdom in a new way?

[1] *See also* John 5:22,23 [2] *See also* Luke 16:9–15

WORRY – A WOEFUL WAY

Yesterday's theme continues. Are you a worrier? Pray that you may find this passage a great encouragement.

LUKE 12:22–34

I'm writing this note on my way back from a funeral, at which 250 people had gathered to mourn and celebrate the life of a 25-year-old man, one of our students at London School of Theology, who had been killed instantly in a collision with a lorry. He was a beautiful Christian, a quiet example of dedicated discipleship, with a life of fruitful service as a youth minister and counsellor stretching in front of him. How we would have loved to add even one more hour to his life – let alone one more year, one more decade.

Events like this could turn us into worriers. 'Let's guard against such ghastly waste and grief as much as possible – and make sure that all the necessary safeguards are in place, before we risk a step into the world,' we think. But Jesus encourages us in the other direction. 'If worry can't add one tiny hour to your life, why do you worry about all the rest?' he says (vs 25,26). He emphasises our value in God's eyes – so much more valuable than the birds whom he feeds; and our beauty in God's eyes – so much more beautiful than the wild flowers which come and go so easily at haymaking. God will certainly feed and clothe creatures in whom he takes such delight – you and me.

But what about Greg, cut down at 25? God's delight in us extends way beyond his desire to provide for our here-and-now earthly life: 'Do not be afraid, little flock, for your Father has been pleased to give you the kingdom' (v 32). We are royalty in his eyes, destined to reign with Christ when the Son of Man comes and this world is transformed by the fullness of God's kingdom. In the meantime, says Jesus, seek the kingdom (v 31), trust your Father (v 32), give away your possessions (v 33), and set your heart on heaven (v 33).

Spend a little time offering up your worries to God … and deepening your sense of trust in him.

ALERTNESS – A BETTER WAY!

When did you last hear a talk on the second coming of Christ? Reflect on whether this doctrine is really 'a living hope'[1] for you, and worship the coming King.

LUKE 12:35–48

The theme of the kingdom of God in yesterday's passage leads on to the theme of this section – the coming of the Son of Man (see v 40). The connection between the two themes is provided in particular by Daniel 7:13 and 14, a most important passage in the background to Jesus' proclamation of the kingdom alongside his designation of himself as 'the Son of Man'. He is the one who, like the 'son of man' in Daniel's vision, 'comes' before God to receive an everlasting 'kingdom', authority and power.

This expectation – of Jesus' 'appearance' in glory and kingly power – is absolutely basic to the New Testament view of the Christian life. Are we watching for him to come? Peter's question in verse 41 is interesting. He's uncertain whether Jesus is still talking privately to his disciples (see how he began, in 12:1), or whether he is now addressing the surrounding crowd as well. It sounds like a message for all – 'be ready for the Lord!' – but Jesus has been talking especially about his 'servants' preparing for him to come (v 37). Who are these? Peter doesn't want his special role as 'the owner of the house' (v 39) to be watered down!

Jesus' reply makes clear that those who know of his future coming have a special responsibility towards those who don't, to help them to be ready for the arrival of the Lord. Peter must have been horrified by the severity of the warning in verses 46 and 47. Do we really take this seriously today? Do we still believe that the Lord is coming urgently, to demand from humanity an account of how we have managed his world? Or are we like the servant in verse 45? Neglect of the expectation of 'the coming of the Lord' leads to preoccupation with present position and power, and is endemic in today's church.

Thank the Lord that he really is 'coming again'. Ask for grace to embrace that faith, truly and deeply.

[1] 1 Pet 1:3

JUDGEMENT IS COMING...

Another 'eschatological' theme: reflect on what you believe, and feel, about 'the judgement of God'. Is this a prominent belief for you? Do you like it? Or not?

LUKE 12:49–59

Jesus believed passionately in the coming judgement of God upon Israel. This is the first thing he speaks about when eventually he reaches Jerusalem,[1] and in chapter 21 he explains his expectation in detail. We believe that he is God's appointed judge for the whole world, not just for Israel,[2] and so it is probably right that in verse 49 we translate his words as 'fire on the earth', rather than 'fire upon the land (of Israel)'. Jesus' appointed role, as Son of God and Saviour, is to cleanse the earth by purifying fire, burning away all that mars this beautiful creation. He longs to fulfil this calling, like a painter longing to restore a damaged picture.

And it's urgent! Jesus uses words drawn from the prophet Micah[3] (vs 52,53), from a passage in which Micah vividly describes the chaos of Israel just before God's judgement falls. There is real horror here, as Jesus appeals to his hearers to settle out of court, before judgement day comes (vs 58,59). For him, it's obvious that judgement is about to happen, as obvious as rain from a cloudy sky (vs 54-56). Probably most of us, if we're honest, do not share his horror.

Some translations omit a 'but' at the beginning of verse 50. What delays God's fiery judgement upon the earth? Jesus' 'baptism' – ie his death for us. God does not want us to perish when he burns the dross from his world. First, his Son will die for us – and the good news will be spread while judgement is delayed.[4] But one day... when the gospel has been fully preached...[5] then finally the world will be cleansed and renewed.[6] Judgement means the final release of the world from all that spoils it.

What effect does this passage have on your feelings about God's judgement? Make a few jottings, and then talk to God about it.

---

[1] *See* Luke 19:41–44 [2] eg Acts 17:31; Rom 2:16 [3] Mic 7:6 [4] 2 Pet 3:9
[5] Mark 13:10 [6] Matt 19:28; Acts 3:21

A DAY AT A TIME

'This day is your last.' Imagine that this message could suddenly appear on your computer screen, announcing the day of your death. Bring your feelings about life's uncertainty to God.

LUKE 13:1–9

This passage speaks deeply to me at the moment, because of the recent death of our student (see the note on Luke 12:22–34). How would he have lived differently, if he had known that he would die suddenly on that morning? There was a day when a squad of Roman soldiers massacred some Galileans visiting Jerusalem to offer sacrifices. And there was a day when a tower collapsed near the pool of Siloam in Jerusalem, killing 18 people. For all these, unknown to them, their lives were to be cut short.

The standard theological view, in Jesus' time, was that illnesses, disasters and premature death were punishment for sin (the view of Job's friends), so it stood to reason that the victims of the disasters reported to Jesus must have been worse sinners than others. But Jesus denies this firmly (vs 3,5).[1] There is no automatic connection, he says, between sin and the mode and timing of death: but there is a direct connection between sin and death! His hearers will certainly die, as we will: maybe suddenly and prematurely, maybe in ripe old age – but die we will.

But there's a way out. 'Unless you repent…': Jesus isn't saying that repentance will save them from collapsing towers and Pilate's violence, but that repentance will save them from eternal death, at whatever age. Repentance, in the sense of a complete change of allegiance, lifestyle and direction, is no easy thing – but nothing else will do. Repentance is the looked-for 'fruit' in the parable in verses 6–9, Jesus' last appeal to the vast crowd around him.[2] It's right at the heart of Jesus' kingdom message.[3] Like a tree bearing its natural fruit, repentance is the fruit we bear when we are living as we are designed to: embracing the kingdom of God, and trusting in his Son. In his kingdom, and through his Son, death is no more.

If this day were to be your last, how would you spend it?

[1] *See also* John 9:1–3 [2] Luke 12:1 [3] *See* Mark 1:15

REPENTANCE AND GRACE

Neither 'repentance' nor 'grace' is mentioned in today's passage, but these are the themes. Write down a definition of the grace of God, and use it as a basis for worship.

LUKE 13:10–17

The scene changes – to a synagogue where Jesus is teaching on the Sabbath – but the themes continue. The synagogue chairman would have no problems with Jesus' parable in verses 6–9, because he knows exactly what kind of 'fruit' God wants. So he also knows exactly what repentance is: it's heartfelt regret before God for every way in which we have failed to keep his Law, and a determination to change by his enabling. It's obvious to him that all kinds of work, including healing chronic spine conditions, should be avoided on the Sabbath, because that is the clear teaching of God's Law. (The Pharisees distinguished between acute medical emergencies, which could be treated on the Sabbath, and chronic long-term conditions, which couldn't.) Jesus, therefore, should repent of his law-breaking.

Jesus points to the grace of care, which all his hearers exercise towards their animals: thirst is not an emergency, but a long-term physical condition which needs treatment every day, including the Sabbath. We can hear Jesus' indignation in verse 16: this 'daughter of Abraham', a prized member of God's covenant with Israel, has been in exile for 18 long years. Isn't it more appropriate to release her on the Sabbath, the covenant day, than on any other?

The point is that, in the kingdom of God, decisions about action are guided not by legalism, but by grace. Jesus is constantly ready to set aside traditional interpretations of law, if grace calls him to. (See the glorious dimensions of this in the story of the Lost Son.)[1] He rejects any interpretation of Scripture which stands in the way of expressing kingdom grace to the lost and the bound. For him, the fourth commandment simply cannot prohibit grace-inspired sacrificial action towards people in need.

Is God calling you in any way to set aside rules/interpretations/customs/taboos for the sake of 'grace to the lost'?

[1] Luke 15:11–32

KINGDOM SURPRISES

Someone has said that Jesus seeks to 'comfort the disturbed and disturb the comfortable'! It's a good summary of his ministry; which would he want to do with you?

LUKE 13:18–30

Verse 18 begins with 'then', linking Jesus' two parables in verses 18–21 with the Sabbath healing and his confrontation with the synagogue chairman. One tiny incident, involving an old lady with chronic scoliosis. But out of this tiny mustard seed, this little spoonful of yeast, the world will be changed! Are we ready for it? The theme of the surprising kingdom continues in verses 22–30, as Jesus leaves the synagogue and continues on his way towards Jerusalem. The question in verse 23 was asked by Jews as they reflected on the surrounding Gentile nations: would God save them too – these millions of pagans? Or would God only save Israel, his covenant people?

Jesus' reply is deeply shocking. He attacks the comfortable, complacent feeling behind the question – the feeling of those who think they're OK because they're the chosen, and who can afford to speculate in a detached way about the fate of the not-chosen. He holds out before his questioner the possibility that he may end up shut out of the kingdom! 'I don't know where you're from,' says the Voice. 'But Lord ... we're yours! We're family with you. We're from Jesus Street.' 'O no, you're not,' comes the reply, 'but they are: that crowd of the not-chosen, piling into the kingdom banquet with Abraham, Isaac and Jacob.'

Not only are the pagans welcomed, but the chosen find themselves shut out. From a Jewish perspective, this shockingly undermines God's covenant commitment to Israel. And what about us? Can we fall into the same complacency? 'Make every effort [literally, "struggle"] to enter the narrow door' (v 24) is Jesus' word for us too. We enter by simple faith, like the woman who trustingly stepped forward (v 12) – but what a journey then begins for us...

Return to the question above, and examine your heart for signs of being 'comfortable'!

JOURNEY'S END IN VIEW

What's been the greatest heartbreak in your life? Gently bring that tender place before the Lord; and prepare to hear about his greatest heartbreak in turn.

LUKE 13:31–35

Luke doesn't want us to forget that all the incidents he describes are stages on a journey, as Jesus moves step by step towards Jerusalem. It's the vital backdrop to everything he describes. Sometimes he reminds us, with a passage like today's, of what's really at stake in this story.

In response to the Pharisees' warning about Herod's plot, Jesus reveals his heart. He shows us (a) his total fearlessness: he will not be put off by a posturing puppet like Herod Antipas of Galilee! – and (b) his absolute determination to fulfil each detail of his ministry, each healing and exorcism, en route to the journey's end (v 32). His determination is fired by (c) his passionate obedience to God's call: in verse 33 he says 'I must press on today and tomorrow and the next day...' – an obedience (d) which will lead to his certain death in Jerusalem, like all the other rejected prophets who have perished there in obedience to God's call (see 9:22,44). Finally, Jesus reveals (e) his heartbroken longing for Jerusalem (vs 34,35). He knows he will be betrayed and crucified there, but he so longs that it could be different!

At one level verse 35 simply looks ahead to Jesus' arrival in Jerusalem,[1] but it has a deeper meaning: Jerusalem will recognise him – truly see him – only when he comes again in glory as Judge, not just as Saviour. Similarly on one level verse 32 looks ahead to the end of the journey in Jerusalem; but more deeply the unusual verb translated 'I will reach my goal' points beyond, to his resurrection and ascension.[2] Tragedy and loss are the route to glory and restoration, for Jesus... and for us!

Jesus knows our heartbreaks, too. There will be glory, beyond the pain. Sit with this truth, and thank God that one day he will wipe away every tear.[3]

[1] Luke 19:38 [2] *See Luke 9:51* [3] Rev 7:17; 21:4

A DIFFICULT GUEST!

Church meetings can get very 'political'. Think back to the last such meeting you attended. Who became 'difficult'? Why? Offer your memories up to God.

LUKE 14:1–14

Now we're with Jesus at a Sabbath dinner party, in the home of a leading, and wealthy, Pharisee. The atmosphere is suspicious (v 1). The sick man may even have been a plant! The issue is the same as before (13:10–17) – will Jesus heal a chronic, long-standing condition on the Sabbath? Answer: yes, unhesitatingly. Jesus' discussion with the Pharisees reveals that he refuses to accept their distinction between acute (emergency) and chronic conditions. If it's OK to rescue man or beast from a pit, then healing is OK, full stop!

Why? Because mercy demands it, and mercy takes precedence over everything else. We see the same principle underlying Jesus' two 'parables', to the guests in verses 7–11 and to his host in verses 12–14. He is remarkably pointed! He comments on the social 'rules' taken for granted in such a gathering: it was an 'honour-shame' culture, in which everyone sought social 'honour' and feared social 'shame'. It was a subtle matter, therefore, to manoeuvre oneself 'up' the table as far as possible, without incurring the shame of presumption.

Jesus cuts through all that. Why not just go straight to the lowest place? Take the place of the shamed? For 'all those who exalt themselves will be humbled, and those who humble themselves will be exalted' (v 11): before God's judgement, all our social manoeuvring is completely insignificant. Similarly, if you're going to give a dinner party, why not invite the people God would invite? Why stick to your friends, in an endless round of mutual social pampering? Once again, Jesus draws out the eternal significance (v 14): you'll be using your wealth as God desires, and God will reward!

What did Jesus' host think of his awkward guest? Jesus breaks the social rules in speaking like this – while telling them that they should break their social rules!

Pray to have God's heart when and if you feel the need to be awkward!

GOD'S SPECIAL GUESTS

Luke – like Jesus – had a special love for 'the poor': the inadequate, the despised, the bypassed. Praise the Lord for his care for 'the poor' – including you!

LUKE 14:15–24

One guest breaks the awkward silence with a pious remark (v 15), designed to gain kudos in that religious company. But behind the question is an unspoken assumption - that only certain people will qualify to eat at the kingdom banquet, and that surely 'we' are among the qualified! In this refined social circle, God was assumed to be at the top of their social pile, the ultimate honoured guest at their feasts. Jesus' parable seems to be about any great social 'event'. It's only because of the comment in verse 15 that we realise he is talking about the kingdom of God! This is the key to understanding the parable: Jesus lets his hearers respond instinctively to it, making their own meaning (see v 35b). What were your gut responses to it, as you read it?

The guests would all have been horrified at the excuses. What rudeness! The host is clearly a man of great status - they would never refuse such an invitation, not even for pressing economic reasons like those given. No, not even because they were on honeymoon! It would be a huge social snub to a powerful man, a source of great shame both to the refusers, and to the inviter. Unthinkable! But it's puzzling that the banquet is then thrown open to the unwashed masses. Why would this host do that? And with such enthusiasm – 'compel them to come in'? Altogether, a very puzzling and unlikely story. What sense does it make?

Maybe, just maybe, Jesus' hearers would catch and consider the message: their wealthy social preoccupations make them deaf to God's invitation, because his kingdom is about breaking down the social distinctions they so carefully preserve - it's about reaching out in love to the lost, the sinners, the unclean.[1]

Respond today to this passage in whatever way it speaks to you right now. Turn its message into prayer.

[1] Look ahead to Luke 15:1,2!

FOLLOWING JESUS

Open your heart to receive a huge challenge from Jesus through this passage today. Commit yourself to being honest before him.

LUKE 14:25–35

This is one of the most challenging passages in the Gospels. The challenge focuses around the three 'cannot be my disciple' sayings in verses 26, 27 and 33. Before looking at these individually it's worth reflecting on the little parable in verses 34 and 35, which summarises them all. Jesus' hearers were used to seeing, beside the roads and fields, piles of broken salt-bearing rock which farmers would use in small quantities as a fertiliser. But over time the rain would leach the salt into the ground, and all the 'goodness' would go out of it. The pile would look OK, but when tested it would turn out to be useless.

Maybe this huge crowd, following Jesus toward Jerusalem (v 25), is like that: they look like disciples, but do they have the fertilising saltiness of true followers? This saltiness has three flavours, the qualities of essential disciples. (a) In their attitude to all other attachments: Jesus takes absolute precedence over family (v 26: love for family must look like hate, compared to their much greater love for Jesus). (b) In their attitude towards all their possessions (v 33): they've given up on them as a focus of interest, so all-absorbing is their focus on Jesus. And (c) in their attitude towards their own lives (v 27): so total is their commitment to Jesus that it is as if their own lives are over and past, like people in Jesus' day carrying crosses to their own execution.

What a stunning demand! Are we equal to this? Jesus says: like a man building a tower or a king going to war, make sure that you can cope with the cost before you get launched! If what we really want is an easy, comfortable life we can't expect to be true followers of Jesus.

Review your discipleship prayerfully before Jesus. Be honest with him as you count the cost. Can you carry on with him, towards Jerusalem?

COME TO THE PARTY!

'I will search for the lost and bring back the strays. I will bind up the injured and strengthen the weak.'[1] What a good Shepherd he is!

LUKE 15:1–10

The scene is set in the first two verses, with the crowd divided into two groups, who operate in contrast to each other in the stories which follow. Tax collecting in the Roman empire was privatised, the contract going to the highest bidder, who would pay the Roman government up front and then recoup from the hapless population. Because of their ill-gotten gains and their perceived collusion with the hated Roman government, tax collectors were despised – but they were among those who had sought John's baptism of repentance,[2] and we have here the picture of high-profile 'sinners' responding to Jesus' message. The Pharisees were unable to share the joy because they had created for themselves a closed religious society, bound by its own traditions, and substituted this for the real kingdom of heaven being inaugurated before their eyes. The church traditions which we (rightly) cherish have a similar power to become so important that they blind us to new things that God is doing in our midst. It is good to remind ourselves that the joy of our fellowship is to be extended, continually, to those who come to Christ.

We see in these parables a God who, by contrast with the Pharisees, is almost obsessively concerned about the one who is lost. It is good to remember this as we falter in our attempts to bring our friends to Christ. He is already searching for each one individually, to bring them into the richly diverse family of his people. Effective evangelism, which respects people as individuals, is at its best when we discover how it is that God is already touching their lives and speak to that. As we join him in his search for our friends, let's make sure that we are ready to welcome them into a community characterised by acceptance, love, joy and forgiveness. It was in such an environment that I and many others first met Christ.

Lord, forgive me when I feel resentment instead of entering into your joy, and teach me and my church to be a welcoming community.

[1] Ezek 34:16 [2] Luke 3:12

A GLORIOUS HOMECOMING

Father, I thank you for the welcome you provide for me every time I come home.

LUKE 15:11–32

There was joy enough for a party when the shepherd found his sheep and the woman her coin. Now we have the same story outline, but significantly developed. It is now a son who is lost. The whole story is now all about family relationships, and is superbly crafted to speak to the grumbling scribes and Pharisees, who never thought of God in these terms. How do you think of God? As a strict authoritarian lawgiver? Or as a father whose love for you never falters, no matter what you may do? When the spendthrift son hit bottom and came to his senses (v 17), he decided to come home and beg to be taken on as a hired servant, doubtless hoping for grudging forgiveness. He probably expected a lecture. What he received was overflowing grace and joy, and complete restoration as his father's son.

Then there is the other son, who had also received his share of the inheritance. While his brother was living it up, he lived a miserable life at home – miserable not because his father was a slave-driver but because he chose never to enjoy his father's love and generosity and cast himself in the role of the slave that his brother had hoped to become (v 29). Like the Pharisees in Jesus' audience, he could not bring himself to share the joy.

There's a little word in the Greek in this story that is easily missed when reading it in English. The father tells the older son (and Jesus tells the Pharisees) that 'we had [literally, "it is necessary"][1] to celebrate'. This Greek word occurs again in the story of Zacchaeus in a similar context: 'I must stay at your house today.'[2] In the parable and in real life it is necessary to celebrate in anticipation of the Messianic banquet[3] whenever a sinner comes to Jesus.

Reflect on your concept of God. May we grasp how wide and long and high and deep is the love of Christ, and know this love that surpasses knowledge.[4]

---

[1] Greek *dei* [2] Luke 19:5 [3] Matt 8:11; Rev 19:9 [4] Eph 3:18,19

LESSON FROM A SCOUNDREL

Lord, please enable me to hear what you want to say to me today about money.

LUKE 16:1–18

This parable is hard to understand if we try to read it as allegory, or if we look for lessons of ethical behaviour. There are, however, parallels between the manager and the prodigal son, brought out by the echoes of vocabulary in the Greek. They both 'squandered' their money and both found themselves in a crisis.[1] Both knew they had a problem, and took matters into their own hands to solve it. At this point the stories diverge. The prodigal manager acted with a stroke of genius, using his master's money, while he still controlled it, to win for himself the friends he would need when he lost his job. The master commended him, not for his good stewardship, but for his shrewdness. Unlike the Pharisees, for whose benefit this story is told, the manager saw the pending disaster and realised the urgency of his situation. What is more, he used what he had for his own salvation. I find Fred Craddock's comment thought-provoking: 'The words ["shrewd" and "clever"] have so commonly been associated with self-serving behaviour, if not ethically questionable behaviour, that it is difficult to speak of a "shrewd saint".'[2] Despite all the inherent dangers of money and possessions, it is possible to use them in a Christian way. (One could extend this line of thinking to admire and emulate those rare Christians who show shrewdness in politics, showing wisdom and integrity as they use the system to advance the kingdom of God.)

Gifts foster relationships. Generosity builds character. We are challenged to think about eternity, to remember that although we cannot take it with us, money can be used to lay up treasure in heaven. The section closes with some direct teaching on our use of money. It matters. How we handle the money we have been entrusted with has eternal consequences.

Lay before the Lord all he has given you in money, talents and time. Ask him to show you creative ways to use his resources for eternal returns.

[1] Luke 15:13; 16:1 where TNIV has 'wasting' [2] *Luke, Interpretation*; Westminster/John Knox Press, 1990

ANOTHER MONEY TRAP

Lord, may the time I spend in your presence open my eyes to the needs of people all around me.

LUKE 16:19–31

Today's reading, an 'example story' rather than a parable, is told with 'extravagant parallelism'.[1] Apparently, versions of it are found in other cultures in the ancient Mediterranean – in one the rich man wore underwear made of Egyptian cotton! It would translate very easily into contemporary Western culture. Luke tells it in the Jewish idiom, complete with the traditional belief that the dead go down to Sheol (the place of the departed).

The anonymous rich man had a serious problem of which he was totally unaware. His comfortable lifestyle inured him to the suffering of the destitute man at his gate, whom he must have seen every day. Like the man who planned to build bigger barns, he lived as if there were no tomorrow.[2] Even after death the rich man had not changed his attitude. He was still as self-centred, and thought he could call upon Lazarus to serve him. But now the barrier which he had put between himself and Lazarus during their lifetimes had become a great chasm. No concession is made to him now. He had his chance.

It would be easy to brush aside stories like this as folk tales, were it not for the prevalence and consistency of the warnings in the Scriptures about the power of money to lead astray. The Old Testament Scriptures, which the Pharisees claimed to live by, are full of injunctions to the rich to help the poor as an expression of their faith in God.[3] Abraham, whom the rich man ironically still considers his father, was known for his hospitality.[4] The New Testament reinforces the command.[5] How we use our money today will determine our eternal future. There is also an urgency, stressed both in this parable and the previous one, to act now. If we wait till tomorrow it may be too late.

'He is no fool who gives what he cannot keep to gain what he cannot lose.'[6]

---

[1] Green, *Luke*, p605 [2] Luke 12:16–21 [3] eg Deut 15:11; Prov 22:9; Isa 58:6,7
[4] Gen 18:1–8 [5] eg 1 Tim 6:17–19 [6] Jim Elliot, 1927–56, missionary to Ecuador

DEALING WITH SIN

Forgive me, Lord, for the things I have said and done that have caused others to stumble.

LUKE 17:1–10

I love the realistic observation that it is inevitable that we will do things that lead others astray – but notice the seriousness of this sin. (For the dire treatment prescribed in verse 2 compare the hyperbole in Matthew 5:30.) To some there is a particular temptation to parade the freedom they have found in the gospel, with more thought to their spiritual superiority than to the danger for others. Some just love heresy. Those of us who teach need to be especially careful.[1]

In dealing with other people's sins we also need to be very careful. That is what the phrase 'watch yourselves' means – the Greek means literally 'pay attention to yourselves'; it is the phrase used by Gamaliel in Acts 5:35. I take this command with what follows as well as with the previous verses, ignoring the paragraph break in the TNIV. We need to be careful about taking specks out of other people's eyes.[2] We all know of disastrous occasions when someone has attempted to confront a 'sinner' in a heavy-handed way. Since Jesus' concern in this whole section is for the weak and marginalised, whatever this text means it cannot mean that a rebuke should cause a rift in the fellowship. There is a reciprocal responsibility for the sinner to repent and for the rebuker to forgive – as many times as it takes. Can you imagine a fellowship in which you never had to worry that someone was critical of your behaviour? In which you knew that everyone loved you unconditionally? In which you knew that everyone had forgiven you? That is what we need to cultivate.

The rest of this section hinges on the Greek word *pistis*, which can mean 'faith', 'faithfulness' or 'trust', or perhaps all three together. Faith does not come in sizes and its power derives not from how much belief we have, but from the one in whom we put our trust.

Pray about the relationships in your fellowship. Is there anyone you need to forgive or to confront? Is there anyone from whom you need to ask forgiveness?

[1] James 3:1–3 [2] Luke 6:41

THE GOOD SAMARITAN

'Temporal mercies are ... doubled and sweetened to us when they are fetched in by the prayers of faith, and returned by the praises of faith.'[1]

LUKE 17:11–19

On the face of it we have here a simple story of healing and thanksgiving. There are so many stories like this in Luke, which, taken singly, seem to have a simple and obvious point to them. We will not go wrong if we take away from today's passage the teaching that Jesus heals, and that he appreciates it when we thank him. However, the context of the surrounding chapters and the mention of the stage in his journey alert us to possibility that Luke is telling us something else as well.

The last time Luke mentioned Jesus' resolute journey towards Jerusalem was at 9:51 (discounting the brief reference at 14:25) when he was also near Samaria, where the disciples wanted to call down fire from heaven because the Samaritans did not welcome him. Now once again he is on the Samaria-Galilee border. This time it is the neediest of the people who appeal to him. They are 'on the edge' in every way: living on the border, banned from the town and from social gatherings. Jesus healed them where they were, 'at a distance' (v 12). So it is significant that one, now cleansed, comes right up to him to thank him publicly.

Luke has left the punch line to the end: 'and he was a Samaritan' (v 16). There has been a gathering emphasis throughout these chapters that the kingdom is being populated – but not with those that the Pharisees would have invited to their party. The glory and honour of the Gentiles are filling it.[2] This had been God's purpose from the beginning, when God promised to Abraham that all peoples of the earth would be blessed through him.[3] As Jesus approaches the cross he reminds the Jews of what they had chosen to ignore throughout their history: they had been chosen in order to carry the light to the Gentiles and to all whom society had marginalised.

Who are the marginalised in your circles? How can you (or your church) become more involved in taking the good news to them?

[1] Matthew Henry's Commentary, Electronic Database, ad loc [2] Rev 21:26
[3] Gen 12:3; cf Isa 51:4

THE COMING KINGDOM

Lord Jesus, amidst all life's uncertainties and crises. help me to keep my eyes fixed on you, my Saviour, Lord and coming King.

LUKE 17:20–37

Throughout the Gospels Jesus' audiences, both disciples and others, are perplexed and confused about the coming of the kingdom of God. This is understandable. The Old Testament has many prophecies about the 'Day of the Lord' which describe the breaking in of God's rule on earth, accompanied by spectacular signs, a terrifying event, a time of doom for the nations, bringing darkness and destruction.[1] And yet Jesus had already indicated that the kingdom was now present.[2] So what about the signs, they wondered, the vindication and the judgement? No doubt, then as now, some were hoping for vindication, others were terrified of judgement.

The TNIV begins this section with 'once', suggesting a break with the previous verses and possibly a different time frame. But the word 'once' is not there in the Greek, and it makes sense to take this teaching about the coming of the kingdom in connection with the thankful Samaritan. The Pharisees' question was wrong-headed, for the kingdom of God was 'in their midst' (TNIV).[3] What looked like a single event in the Old Testament will turn out to be a protracted series of events – like a mountain range, which, seen from a distance, looks like a single mountain.

Before the final day of the Lord could come it was necessary that he should suffer and die. If the Pharisees' question implied that they were afraid of missing the final establishment of the kingdom, they need not have worried. When he finally returns in glory no one will miss it.[4] In the meanwhile, the challenge to us is to be faithfully living out the kingdom values, careful not to be totally absorbed in the business of this world. His return will be sudden and there will be no time to look back.

Two questions: Do I see God's activity in the present? Am I ready for Jesus' return? May today's passage help me to think Christianly about these things.

[1] Ezek 30:3; Joel 1:15; Zeph 2:1–3 [2] Luke 11:20 [3] NIV has 'within you'; the Greek could mean either [4] Rev 1:7

TWO LESSONS IN PRAYER

'May it be the real I that speaks. May it be the real Thou that I speak to.'[1]

LUKE 18:1–14

'Increase our faith!' the disciples had begged (17:5). Can unanswered prayer be God's way of increasing our faith? Think how Jesus treated the Syro-Phoenician woman before holding her up as an example of faith.[2] When Lazarus died, he purposely stayed away from Bethany for two days.[3] It would seem that Jesus values our persistence, and we can be confident that when our prayers are not answered it is not because they have not been heard.

Jesus' teaching about prayer asks us to extrapolate from relationships we know to 'how much more' we can expect from our heavenly Father. Prayer in Luke's Gospel is all about our relationship with the Father, who will not give us a snake when we ask for a fish.[4] The uncaring judge finally gives the widow what she wants because he is afraid he is going to end up with a (figurative) black eye (translated 'attack me', v 5). God bears with our hammering at his door and answers in his perfect time. In the meanwhile our faithful persistence deepens our faith. We may also learn that he is trying to get through to us, too. Philip Yancey writes: 'When Peter went on a roof to pray (Acts 10) he was mainly thinking about food. Little did he know that he would descend from the roof convicted of racism and legalism.'[5]

If prayer depends on our relationship with God, we must get that right. The Pharisee who prayed about himself had missed Jesus' point about the master and the slave in chapter 17.[6] The tax collector had a true understanding of who he was in the sight of God. Such humility goes against the grain for most of us, and it's easy to mouth the tax collector's prayer without sincerely seeing ourselves as sinners. I think we need to take a little time to let this sink in. Without his cross there is no crown.

Who, or what, have you given up praying for? Why?

[1] CS Lewis, *Letters to Malcolm*, Fontana, 1966, p109 [2] Mark 7:25–30 [3] John 11:6–7,21 [4] Luke 11:11 [5] *Prayer, Does it Make any Difference?*, Zondervan, 2006, p153 [6] Luke 17:7–10

A STUDY IN CONTRASTS

Lord Jesus, teach me your values and help me to orient my life around them.

LUKE 18:15–30

The crowd is pressing round Jesus with needs of all sorts. Brilliant parables are falling from his lips. His teaching is intriguing. And pushing their way through the crowd come women with babies. Of course they are a nuisance. They are also the perfect visual aid to all that Jesus had been teaching about our relationship with our heavenly Father. Babies are totally dependent, and their relationship with their parents matters more to them than anything else.

A rich man, who must have been in the crowd listening to Jesus' teaching about money, now steps forward. He has lived a decent life, and was possibly included in the members of the crowd 'who were confident of their own righteousness'[1] for whose benefit Jesus had told the parable of the Pharisee and the tax collector. Although the story fits exactly with what Paul would later teach about grace,[2] that does not seem to be the point here, since Jesus replies by telling him that he needs to do something further: in effect, to love God with all his heart by getting rid of his idolatry of money and to love his neighbour as himself by giving his money to the poor. Jesus had put his finger on the very issue that was keeping him from becoming a disciple. He is cornered, and turns to join the rich whom the Messiah has 'sent empty away'.[3]

The story of the rich man, and especially the memorable epigram that follows it (v 25), is disturbing. We should remember that this is the record of our Lord's dealing with one particular individual. The lawyer who asked the same question[4] got a different answer. That said, we must allow Jesus to speak to us personally too, and allow him to show us the things in our lives that hinder us in following him.

'Where your treasure is, there your heart will be also.'[5]

[1] Luke 18:9 [2] eg Eph 2:8 [3] Luke 1:53, AV [4] Luke 10:25 [5] Luke 12:34

SEEING AND BELIEVING

Thank Jesus Christ for the depth of his suffering for you and for me. It is almost more than we can bear. It was the only way.

LUKE 18:31–43

This is the third time that Jesus had spoken to his disciples about what was about to happen to him in Jerusalem. The first occasion is recorded immediately after Peter's confession of him as the Christ,[1] and repeated later in the same chapter,[2] after which the disciples immediately showed how little they understood by falling into an argument about who was going to be the greatest. Jesus responded then, as here, with the object lesson of a little child. They still do not understand. It is the women at the tomb[3] who, reminded by the angels about Jesus' words that it was necessary for him to be crucified and to rise again, showed the first glimmer of understanding and relayed the news to the still sceptical disciples. Then, appearing to the couple on the Emmaus road, Jesus explained that it was necessary for this to have happened, and their eyes were opened.[4] Before we blame them for their obtuseness, we might ask ourselves how often we hear only what we want to hear, and how selective we are in reading the Scriptures.

The first time Jesus spoke to the disciples about his impending death he told them how he was to be handed over to the Jewish authorities. Luke is careful to blame not only the Jews; this time it is the Gentiles who will mock him and kill him, a point that Luke makes again in Acts 4:27, where both Herod and Pontius Pilate, with the Gentiles and the people of Israel, are equally held to account.

By contrast, the blind beggar knew that he was blind, the increasing crescendo of his shouts conveying his desperation. Jesus opens his eyes – while the privileged do not see. It is sometimes easier for the outcasts – poor, crippled and blind – to understand the kingdom of God, with its great reversal of values, than it is for the rest of us.

Why do you think Jesus asked the blind man what he wanted? What do you want him to do for you?

---

[1] Luke 9:20–22 [2] Luke 9:44 [3] Luke 24:6–8 [4] Luke 24:26 (TNIV 'have to...'),31

MORE THAN MEETS THE EYE

'I sought the Lord, and afterward I knew / he moved my soul to seek him, seeking me.'[1]

LUKE 19:1–10

All through this section we have been presented with contrasting pairs of characters: the younger and older son, the rich man and Lazarus, the Pharisee and the tax collector. Zacchaeus' story beautifully counterpoises that of the rich ruler in the last chapter,[2] and shows how a camel may indeed go through the eye of a needle! Zacchaeus needed no prompting to part with his money. Whereas the rich man went away sad, Zacchaeus welcomed Jesus with joy. This anecdote brings full circle the theme with which this section of Luke began. Chapter 15 began with the Pharisees criticising Jesus for dining with 'tax collectors and sinners'; in the story of Zacchaeus, a 'chief' tax collector (perhaps a district superintendent), they are at it again.

Jesus' riposte is the same as before: the Son of Man came to seek and to save the lost. But in this story, who is searching for whom? Zacchaeus thought he was looking for Jesus, only to find out that Jesus was looking for him. He wanted to know who Jesus was, only to discover that Jesus knew who he was. And there is a further reason why Jesus invited himself to Zacchaeus' house. Set in Jesus' final days of ministry, with his crucifixion imminent, this incident is phrased in the language of the coming kingdom of God. There is the urgency of the words 'today' and 'immediately'. And lurking in the text is that little Greek word of Messianic significance, *dei*, 'it is necessary' (v 5). Something greater than the conversion of one tax collector is going on.

The risen Christ continues to seek and to save. An encounter with him reorders our priorities. It is still urgent to respond to him.[3] My prayer is that all who read these notes may experience his love and enter into the joy of radical discipleship.

Reflect on your own experience with the risen Christ, and the times when he has sought you out. Thank him with joy!

[1] Anonymous, c 1878 [2] Luke 18:18–25 [3] Heb 3:7

LIVING BETWEEN THE TIMES

'Teach me to live with a grateful heart, and as Thou hast today come anew into my soul so abide in me continually, till ... I may see Thee face to face.'[1]

LUKE 19:11–27

This story follows on from the conversion of Zacchaeus. It takes place in the same location, and it's part of Jesus' way of managing expectations. If a tax collector can find salvation, then the kingdom of God must be on its way – and it will happen here in Jerusalem – or so the reasoning goes (v 11).

Jesus' parable begins to prepare the disciples for the idea that he is about to leave them, and that he won't become King until his return (v 12); that he will in fact be rejected (v 14); and that there will be a task for the disciples to be engaged in until his return – profitable service. This story is different from the parable of the talents.[2] There, the focus is on how we use God's gifts; in this passage, it's all about attitudes. The attitude of the citizens is not to want the King at all (v 14) – Jesus' kingdom will provoke hostility and opposition. The attitude of one of the slaves is to do nothing with what he's been given (v 20) – whereas to believe in Jesus' kingdom presupposes that his followers will live it out. Christians live 'between the times' – knowing that, in Jesus, the kingdom has been inaugurated, but that it only finds its completion in a new heavens and a new earth. In between, Christians are called to live lives of service, making the most of what they've been given. (We aren't, interestingly, told anything about the fate of the other seven slaves!)

The sting in the tail of all this is that there is also judgement on those who reject the King (v 27). Our calling is therefore also to share the good news of the kingdom so that others may find faith, and not suffer the fate of the rebel citizens.

What does 'living between the times' entail for me? Am I investing what God has entrusted to me? Where is God calling me to make changes in my life?

---

[1] Cecil John Wood, *A Form of Spiritual Communion*, Melanesia, 1916
[2] Matt 25:14–30

REVOLUTIONARY COLT

'Ride on, ride on in majesty; / in lowly pomp ride on to die. / Bow thy meek head to mortal pain; / then take, O God, thy power and reign.'[1]

LUKE 19:28–44

A revolutionary leader wants to give a clear message to his followers about who he is and what he stands for. He arranges with some villagers to borrow a young donkey and ride it into the city – and the manner of his entry into the city itself becomes a prophetic act. Jesus knew what he was doing. Zechariah[2] foretold the coming of a Messianic figure riding 'on a colt, the foal of a donkey'. As he enters Jerusalem, he is greeted with words from Psalm 118 – the psalm sung by and to pilgrims. But the meaning of the psalm is transformed, for the disciples are hailing the man on the donkey as the Messiah, the promised one, whom they have recognised through his marvellous acts (v 37). The significance of all this is not lost on the Pharisees (v 39), but Jesus humours them: 'Keep my disciples quiet, and the rocks and stones will join in!' The whole of creation joins in the recognition of the Coming One.

From exultation to dereliction, as Jesus weeps for Jerusalem. He foresees the destruction of the city and Temple by the Romans in AD 70. The Jewish people neither recognised what would bring them peace – the shalom of God (v 42) – nor did they recognise that the Messiah's visitation which they anticipated was in fact taking place (v 44). They'd missed both God's peace and the author of peace.

Our own concern for the well-being of the places in which we live can be informed by Jesus' approach. Our prayers must start with the desire that God's wholeness and peace might prevail, but will also be informed by the desire for our friends and neighbours to have their eyes opened to the presence of Jesus in his people and in his church.

Pray for and seek the good of the city or place in which you live[3] – and pray for the peace of Jerusalem.

---

1 HH Milman, 1827 2 Zech 9:9 3 *Cf* Jer 29:7

TEMPLE TACTICS

'All the people hung on his words.'[1] Lord Jesus, may I not just be fascinated by your teaching, but moved to put it into practice.

LUKE 19:45 – 20:8

One of the big questions of our time is the nature of authority. It's characteristic of our culture that people question traditional authority – Parliament, the Law, the church – and want to see some justification as to why a particular authority should be thought to be legitimate. We need convincing that a leader's authority is worth taking notice of.

In today's passage, Jesus demonstrates why his authority has stood the test of time. He cleanses the Temple of those who were profiteering there, and speaks and acts with righteous anger in the name of God (vs 45,46). By contrast, he exhibits a quiet and spellbinding authority in his teaching (v 48). He's enigmatic when the source of his authority is subject to direct challenge and questioning by the chief priests and teachers of the Law (20:1–8). It's a brilliant response, impaling them on the horns of a dilemma: 'Are you going to accept John the Baptist's teaching as coming from God, or criticise him and run the risk of unpopularity? You know you have no answer!' They can't respond. Here is a teacher to be reckoned with.

One reason I follow Jesus Christ is his authority and the way he exercises it. He's not afraid of power, but exercises it justly. He's comfortable teaching the crowds in the Temple and engaging with them. He knows when to answer, and when to keep silent. So, for Christians, the challenge is to discover the Jesus way of operating in the myriad situations we find ourselves in. For our society, disillusioned by politicians and suspicious of inherited power, discovering the radical authority of Jesus would make a huge difference to the way we live.

Are you in a position of authority? How can you exercise power better, for the good of those for whom you have responsibility – at work, in church, in the community?

[1] Luke 19:48

OFFICIAL HEALTH WARNING

'Christ is made the sure foundation; Christ the head and cornerstone.'[1]

LUKE 20:9–18

Ever overheard a conversation where someone is talking about you in not exactly glowing terms? It's a pretty pointed parable that Jesus tells the people here, with the scribes and chief priests as the unflattered audience. Unlike some of the parables, it has to be treated as an allegory: the vineyard is the people of God; the tenants are the leaders of the people; the slaves are the prophets; and the son and heir is the expected Messiah. The picture is of the continual apostasy of the Old Testament people of God and their rejection of the prophets (vs 10-12). What is so bold in Jesus' story is, of course, the reference to his own approaching passion and death (vs 13-15). It shocks the people - 'God forbid' (v 16) is a strong expression in the Greek - and stirs the chief priests to want to do away with Jesus (v 19).

The story of salvation is full of reversals - life through death, joy through tribulation - and Jesus concludes his story by quoting (v 17) the great reversal of Psalm 118:22, a favourite text in the early church. The cornerstone is architecturally obscure, but it is fundamental to the building. Jesus takes this Old Testament thought and applies it to himself. That which would be left in the quarry, unused and unusable, is made into the centrepiece. Jesus, despised and rejected, will take centre stage in God's plan of salvation, a salvation which indeed consists in good news for rejects.

Stones can be more than decorative, too. Fall over one, or have one fall on you, and it causes damage (v 18). People may reject Jesus, but it will lead to their own rejection and judgement. The chief priests recognise where this is going - one more step on the road to the cross.

Are you seeking to share your faith with someone who seems constantly to reject God? Pray for breakthrough in their lives – that they'll find the Cornerstone, not the stumbling stone.

[1] JM Neale, 1818–66

HEADS OR TAILS?

'The church must be reminded that it is not the master or the servant of the state, but rather the conscience of the state.'[1]

LUKE 20:19–26

Christians have often argued about how our faith relates to the political authorities. Can the State require us to bear arms? To pay taxes? To deny our faith? Jesus' teaching here, in response to a trick question, indicates the beginnings of an answer further explored by Paul[2] and John.[3] Palestine under the Roman occupation was full of resentment – why should we pay tribute to the Emperor? To discredit Jesus would be easy – if he answered in favour of paying taxes to Caesar, he was a traitor to the Jews; if he answered against paying taxes, he was a lawbreaker.

The questioners start with simulated honesty (v 20), flattery (v 21), and a seemingly straightforward question (v 22): is it lawful to pay the tax? Jesus' reply both confounds his critics and lays the foundations for the Christian theology of the State! There is a legitimate role for the State – even the intolerant State – which means that the follower of Jesus is not exempt from paying taxes and good citizenship: 'Give back to Caesar what is Caesar's' (v 25). However, we are citizens of another kingdom, and the kingdom of God takes priority over our national cultural identities: 'to God what is God's' (v 25). Working those headlines into a full-blown theology takes a little longer. It does mean that the State can make legitimate demands on us. It also means that there will be circumstances when we must obey God, rather than human laws.[4] For Christians in many parts of the world, such as Nigeria and Pakistan, these are real life-or-death choices.

What is government like in your locality? Your country? How might you be praying creatively for your elected leaders in church? Are there Christians involved in politics who need your support? How about a prayer focus in church one Sunday soon?

'Almighty God, to whom we must all give account: guide with your Spirit our leaders and politicians; that they may seek in all their purposes to enrich our common life. Amen.'[5]

[1] Anon [2] Rom 13:1–7; Titus 3:1,2 [3] Rev 13:1–10 [4] Acts 5:29 [5] 'Collect for Social Justice', *Common Worship*, Church House Publishing, 2005

DEAD OR ALIVE?

'Jesus lives! – your terrors now / can no more, O death, appal us; / Jesus lives! – by this we know / you, O grave, cannot enthral us. Alleluia!'[1]

LUKE 20:27–40

More controversy for Jesus; this time with the Sadducees. They were the conservative aristocrats of the priestly party, who sought to uphold the teachings of the Torah (the Law of Moses). They taught that there is no resurrection, and tried to ridicule Jesus with another trick academic question. The custom of levirate marriage had more or less died out in Jesus' time. It was a way of keeping a man's family line going if he died childless (v 28). Now, based on an imaginary story of seven brothers, all of whom died, the Sadducees try to reduce belief in resurrection to an absurdity (vs 29–33). Rationalists today like Richard Dawkins still try in a similar way to discredit anything supernatural.

Jesus' response is to reshape their dull, flat ideas of resurrection. It's not just more of the same old life on earth, as some Jews believed. It's qualitatively different (v 35); it's eternal (v 36), and it will be lived in different bodies (v 36). And, for the Sadducees, the clincher is that it's presaged in the Torah (v 37).

We probably regret that Jesus wasn't a bit more specific about what it will be like! Personally, I find it hard to imagine the new heavens and new earth. The promise of resurrection is sure, but we shall have to wait for the reality of the experience. It comes in the category of puzzling reflections in a mirror.[2]

The funeral service speaks of the 'sure and certain hope of the resurrection to eternal life'.[3] Are there friends or family members with whom you're in contact who need to know that sure and certain hope, for themselves or for their nearest and dearest? If so, Jesus' words are words of encouragement and affirmation. Take time today for yourself, too, to thank God that in Jesus' death and resurrection is the promise of eternal life for all who believe.

Think how you could share with someone creatively about a relationship with God beyond death.

[1] After CF Gellert, 1715–69 and FE Cox, 1812–97, alt [2] 1 Cor 13:12
[3] *Common Worship*

QUESTIONS AND WARNINGS

'Hail to the Lord's anointed, great David's greater Son!'[1]

LUKE 20:41 – 21:4

Jesus sets a riddle to the teachers of the Law and chief priests. It was a conundrum which strikes at the heart of the question of who Jesus is (which is where the controversy in this chapter started – in 20:2). Everyone knew that the Messiah was to be David's Son.[2] But Psalm 110 has David addressing the Messiah as Lord (vs 42-44). How could that be? The theological answer is, of course, Jesus' own pre-existence: he was with God from the very beginning, but incarnate as a descendant of David. Jesus has authority because he is the Messiah, who was there before David, but is happy to own the title 'David's Son'. He also transforms that title from contemporary popular understanding – a liberator who would overthrow the Romans – to a different kind of Messiah, whose power is exercised through weakness.

A second cameo has Jesus voicing his criticism of the way these theologians behave (vs 45-47). Strutting around, desiring recognition and wanting the best seats in the house, as well as taking money from widows – Jesus' description of them isn't pretty. A good point to check our own attitudes: do we, if we're church leaders or managers, public figures or people of influence, mirror any of this sort of behaviour? Does the Christian calling to be a servant leader make a practical difference in our lives? Notice Jesus' condemnation of them (v 47)! Scene 3 is one of the classic passages on Christian giving. A simple scene – the rich ostentatiously making their contributions to the Temple treasury, while the poor widow sneaks her gift into the pot. It would transform giving to charities and in our churches if we could grasp the simplicity of giving wholeheartedly, rather than out of our abundance (which often means the leftovers).

Lord, give me the eyes to see you as Messiah, the humility not to be served but to serve, and the sacrificial commitment to place all I have at your disposal.

[1] J Montgomery, 1771–1854 [2] Matt 1:1

DANGEROUS RUMOURS

'"Awesome architecture!" Jesus replies, "I tell you, all this'll be like a Lego tower with a toddler – flat, not one stone left on another."'[1]

Jesus has spoken of the end of the Temple previously, in chapter 19. Now a remark about the beauty of it leads him to speak more about its destruction (vs 5,6). The confusing thing about his words in this chapter is that some of what he says is about the destruction of Jerusalem, and some is about the end of the world. The language is apocalyptic – it hides the truth in mysterious and sometimes incomprehensible images.

What links the end of Jerusalem and the coming of the Son of Man is judgement. Jesus is asked for a sign (v 7), but he is insistent that there is no one sign of judgement. Instead, he tells the disciples to look for a number of things: false Messiahs (v 8); wars between nations (vs 9,10); natural disasters (v 11); persecutions (vs 12-19). We are encouraged to consider that these might always be signs of God's judgement at work – indeed, that his judgement works throughout human history[2] – and that these experiences will always be part of the lot of the church.

There are Christians who want to produce a timetable of the end of the world. Jesus gives them no encouragement. What is clear is that the Temple was destroyed in AD 70; Christian history has been peppered with the same sort of pattern of events; and we are to expect a future coming of the Son of Man as the culmination of all things (v 27). Some churches are so preoccupied with this teaching that it is a constant theme; others relegate it to just one annual sermon, usually on Advent Sunday! We need a consciousness of God as judge and saviour that informs our understanding of history and teaches us to pray for the world and work for God's justice more creatively.

'Almighty God, purify our hearts and minds, that when your Son Jesus Christ comes again as judge and saviour we may be ready to receive him, who is our Lord and our God.'[3]

---

[1] Mark 13:1,2 from Rob Lacey, *The Street Bible*, Zondervan, 2002
[2] Rom 1:18–32 [3] 'Alternative Collect of Advent', *Common Prayer*

THE COMING SON OF MAN

'Jesus of Nazareth was conscious of a vocation: he would embody in himself the returning and redeeming action of the covenant God.'[1]

LUKE 21:20–38

Luke spells out for us what Jesus had to say about the end of Jerusalem. It's impossible to underestimate the effect that this destruction was to have on the Jewish people. Jesus' words evoke the horrors of the siege that took place some 30 years later (vs 20-24). But God's judgement on Israel is not the last of his judgements: there is a universal judgement to come, described in verse 25 onwards. Jesus speaks of signs and portents, and picks up the words of Daniel 7:13 about the coming of the Son of Man. In the end, it's about the culmination of all things being in Jesus, who took for himself the title 'Son of Man'. It's about God in Jesus Christ.

The application of the parable of the fig tree (vs 29-33) is puzzling. There's a simple point – leaves are a sign of summer; the events Jesus has prophesied are a sign of judgement and the coming kingdom. What then, of the words 'this generation will certainly not pass away' (v 32)? Jesus is probably indicating that the 'times of the Gentiles' (v 24) are being ushered in, and the generation of the Gentiles – ie the Christian church – will be around until the end.

How, then, should we live in the light of all this? Jesus urges his disciples not to waste their time (through drunkenness), nor to worry away their time (through the cares of the world), but to be alert in our living, ready to stand before the Son of Man. Do we measure up to what Jesus is calling us to do and to be here? The huge busyness of twenty-first-century daily life can easily blunt the radical nature of Jesus' call to discipleship. Perhaps we need more seriousness about our commitment to live our lives with eternity in mind.

'O Lord our God, ... keep us faithful as we await the coming of your Son ... that ... he may ... find us active in his service and joyful in his praise.'[2]

---

1 NT Wright, *Jesus and the Victory of God*, SPCK, 1996, p653
2 Post-Communion Prayer for Advent I, *Common Worship*

NEXT TIME IN HEAVEN?

'Because there is one loaf, we, who are many, are one body, for we all partake of the one loaf.'[1] Thank God for the unity of all true believers in Christ.

LUKE 22:1–23

Jesus warns us that Satan is a murderer and a liar.[2] He first appears in the Bible as a snake, and latterly as a bloated dragon bent on destruction. The person who flirts with the snake may be devoured by the dragon. 'Then Satan entered Judas' (v 3). What terrible words – and what a terrible warning!

Apparently this Passover supper did not include a lamb, since God had himself provided the Lamb.[3] Jesus anticipates the fulfilment of this supper in the kingdom of God (v 16) and he expects that each time we re-enact the Last Supper we should also anticipate its fulfilment[4] – yet this aspect of communion is scarcely mentioned in our liturgies. Everything we Christians most long for lies on the other side of the grave, and it is that expectation which deprives death of its sting and its victory.

Throughout history, different groups of Christians have attached their own significance to the words 'this is my body', and have too often spilt each other's blood in the process. That very clever woman Queen Elizabeth I of England, writing during the heat of the Reformation, said: ''Twas God the Word that spake it; / He took the bread and brake it; / And what the Word did make it; / That I believe and take it.' As we celebrate the Lord's Supper the focus of our attention must be Jesus' words in the Gospels and 1 Corinthians 11, which transcend our differences within the Christian family; for it is there that our unity lies. It is a great scandal that Christians have often allowed our arguments about the feast to deflect our focus from Jesus and to weaken the unity that Christ died for and that is symbolised in the one loaf.[5]

Christians can afford to look death in the face because we look beyond it. Next time you take communion, anticipate its fulfilment in Jesus' heavenly victory banquet.

[1] 1 Cor 10:17 [2] John 8:44 [3] Gen 22:8; John 1:29 [4] 1 Cor 11:26 [5] John 17:11; 1 Cor 10:17

THE LION AND THE LAMB

What ambitions do you have? What kind of greatness do you aspire to? 'In your relationships with one another, have the same attitude of mind Christ Jesus had.'[1]

LUKE 22:24–38

This passage about greatness and servanthood goes to the heart of Christ's nature. In Revelation the mysterious person who is worthy to unroll the scroll is announced as the Lion of Judah – but he turns out to be a sacrificial Lamb. How can the centre of holiness and power be that symbol of utter weakness, a dead Lamb? How can holy wrath and divine love come together? Only through a sacrificial, atoning death.

But this ultimate heavenly mystery is intensely practical. Despite three years with Jesus the disciples could not understand how divine power could work through human weakness. Status was what they wanted, but Jesus reminds them that, though one day they will enjoy an honoured place in his kingdom, now is the time for humble service, following his example (vs 26,27).

Suddenly Jesus turns to Simon with an urgent warning. Temptation and trial lie ahead, but Jesus has anticipated it in prayer (vs 31,32). The purpose of trial here, as elsewhere, is to show us our real selves, and out of that to enable us to depend on God and strengthen each other. When Jesus first commissioned the disciples in Galilee they worked in friendly, hospitable surroundings, but now that has all changed. Their Master is to be 'numbered with the transgressors' (v 37), so they need to be prepared – but once again they misunderstand, thinking Jesus is talking about armed resistance (v 38)! This raises practical issues for Christians in difficult environments. There are times when there is an openness to the gospel, but that is not the case in many parts of the world today where, to quote Revelation, 'the devil has gone down to you … filled with fury.'[2] We have much to learn from Christians who have suffered severe persecution and through it grasped how to trust in the Lord and not themselves.

Pray for all who face hostility or temptation today, especially any you have heard about recently.

1 Phil 2:6 2 Rev 12:12

THE POWER OF A LOOK

'But if we were more discerning with regard to ourselves, we would not come under ... judgement,'[1] said Paul. Start today with some healthy self-criticism.

LUKE 22:39–62

How do we imagine the day of judgement? In CS Lewis' children's book, *The Last Battle*, the judgement of each creature takes place as it looks directly into the eyes of Aslan, the Lion, and reacts with instant love and joy or hatred and fear. So too with Peter. One glance from Jesus (v 61), and he is overwhelmed with bitter weeping and regret. His former bombast and bravado, the declarations of undying faithfulness, have been exposed as empty words. As Simeon said in his prophecy over the infant Jesus, through him 'the thoughts of many hearts will be revealed.'[2] Thank God, along with this revelation of sin there is also a revelation of grace – in forgiveness for the truly repentant.

There is something deeply contemptible about the way the authorities arrest Jesus – the bribery and the kiss of Judas, the armed thugs arresting a harmless man, the darkness that envelops everything that happens.

Each of us has at some time faced the future with dread, when we would have done anything to avoid a confrontation, a trial or suffering of some kind. It is as though all such human foreboding was summed up in this one event as Jesus took on himself the suffering of a world in pain and pleaded for some way out of the next day's trials. Eventually, he submits to the will and purposes of his Father, and is strengthened by an angel in the midst of his anguish (vs 41–44). Twice Jesus exhorts the disciples to pray that they might not fall into temptation (vs 40,46), and earlier he had prayed that Peter's faith might not fail.[3] This is a strong reminder about the power of temptation, and our continuing need to pray for ourselves and our fellow Christians.

Pray that you will not fall into temptation.

---

[1] 1 Cor 11:31 [2] Luke 2:35 [3] Luke 22:32

LET JUSTICE FLOW

'The LORD is known by his acts of justice; the wicked are ensnared by the work of their hands.'[1] Take time to worship God for his unswerving justice.

LUKE 22:63 – 23:12

There is something depressingly familiar about these soldiers (22:63-65). Their descendants are alive and well in most countries. Beat the prisoner up a bit to show who is in charge and get a little sadistic fun out of it. Herod hoped for the same thing at a later stage (23:11). Today still, many Christians and other prisoners of conscience experience terrible atrocities at the hands of people contemptuous of justice, or who believe they are instruments of the divine will. There is a voluminous literature about the trial of Jesus, but broadly speaking there was a desire to keep to the letter of the law, for example by not starting the trial proper until daybreak, while breaching the Law when the need arose, with the false accusations in verse 2. Legalism at its worst!

How could Jesus answer the question, 'Are you the Christ?'? If his enemies had not understood what kind of Messiah he was during the many hours he taught and ministered in the Temple and elsewhere, how would they understand now? Come to that, do we understand what kind of Christ we worship? Do we practise that divine weakness which overcomes human power? It is often suggested that communism in Russia was brought down by the faithful prayers of the old ladies who continued to attend worship through the darkest days of persecution. They seemed to be no threat to the regime because they were too weak. In our church, family and business lives, have we learnt their lesson? By contrast, the family of Herod the Great illustrates how power can destroy and corrupt people. This Herod was debauched, superstitious and tormented by guilt, like his father. He wanted to know if this could possibly be John the Baptist risen from the dead.[2] Silence from Jesus was the only appropriate response.

Let us make sure we act justly today, at home at work, at church; and let us take our stand against injustice wherever we find it.

[1] Ps 9:16 [2] Luke 9:7–9

WHAT'S GOING ON HERE?

Take a few minutes to thank God that Jesus has experienced for us the whole range of human wickedness.

A good geologist can look at the vegetation growing on a landscape and deduce the kind of soil which lies beneath it, the way the soil was formed and by what kind of rocks, and explain their formation in geological history. We need that kind of analysis to understand what is going on in this crucial passage. Why can Pilate not release Jesus and tell the authorities to go away? Why are the authorities so enraged with Jesus? The charge of blasphemy is the excuse for their rage, but the rage came first. What caused the rage? Is it reasonable to hate someone whose every action is a good one? Something pushes us beyond rational explanation to see the spiritual forces in humanity that make us either worship goodness or hate it. The demand for crucifixion reveals a terrible, intense hatred of Jesus that can be satisfied by nothing but utter degradation and torture. Later Roman persecutors such as Nero showed the same rage.

There is an extraordinary irony in the story of Barabbas. Here is a man, whose name, according to a likely variant reading of Matthew 27:16, was also Jesus; and Barabbas means son (*bar*) of the father (*abba*)! Apparently he had tried, like many others, to liberate his country by armed rebellion from the Roman yoke (v 19). His deserved death is instead suffered by the other Jesus, Son of the Father, an exchange that is symbolic of our salvation. At the beginning of his ministry Jesus rejected the temptation to use human power to accomplish his work.[1] Barabbas, and all such liberators since, illustrate why. 'Flesh gives birth to flesh, but the Spirit gives birth to spirit,' said Jesus.[2] Our salvation is not secured by more wars, more politics, more elections, more science. Only the incarnation, death, resurrection and ascension of Jesus can achieve that.

Let us love people with all their ugliness and sin as God does, and be grateful that he has redeemed us despite our unworthiness.

[1] Luke 4:5–8 [2] John 3:6

TAKE UP THE CROSS

'If we died with him, we will also live with him.'[1] Lord, as I read, stir my heart again to follow you.

LUKE 23:26–46

So here is Simon, up for the festival from Cyrene in North Africa, who unwittingly and unwillingly becomes the first person to 'take up his cross and follow' Jesus. He may later have become a Christian and father of two Christian sons.[2] It was a tough introduction to the faith.

We do a great disservice to the gospel if we understate the reality of judgement and the holiness of God. The affluence and arrogance of the Western world tempt us to think that everything will continue as it is – but it will not. Jesus' warning to the women of Jerusalem (vs 28–31) was terribly fulfilled within a generation. Judgement is real, but so too is forgiveness. I am writing these notes on the anniversary of the abolition of the slave trade. On the television I have just seen the descendant of a rich English slave trader asking forgiveness from the descendant of a slave. It must have cost the latter to say he forgave the unutterable wrong done. We are never more like our Master than when we forgive those who have hurt us. It is wonderful to see how the dying words of Jesus were taken up by disciples under persecution, such as Stephen and Paul.[3]

Theological discussion happens in the strangest places, and often when most needed. The words of Jesus to the dying thief (vs 43) are a wonderful consolation to all of us whose faith is small – no bigger than a mustard seed, perhaps, but enough.[4] Nothing so illustrates the mystery of the incarnation as the crucifixion, where an event of cosmic significance also appears as no more than a passing event: three hours of darkness, a torn curtain, a huddled group of bewildered women, a frightened soldier, yet to the eye of faith the turning point of history.[5]

If you are struggling to forgive someone – just do it, and may God help you.

[1] 2 Tim 2:11 [2] See Mark 15:21 [3] Acts 7:60; 2 Tim 4:16 [4] Luke 17:6
[5] Gal 4:4,5

DARKNESS AT NOON

'Well might the sun in darkness hide, / and shut his glories in, / when Christ, the mighty Maker, died, / for man, the creature's, sin.'[1] Think about the significance of this unnatural darkness.

LUKE 23:47–56

The darkness which surrounded Jesus' death was not an eclipse, but it created an ominous sense of unease in the bystanders as they 'beat their breasts' (v 48). No good could come from this terrible treatment of a good man. Luke does not draw any conclusions from the tearing of the Temple curtain, but such an uncanny event heightened the sense of awe. The author of Hebrews would see profound meaning in it.[2] Out of the darkness the simple trust of Jesus in his Father caused the Gentile centurion to praise God for this 'righteous' (and hence innocent) man who had just breathed his last (v 47). In Luke's sequel, the Acts of the apostles, many Gentiles (including another centurion)[3] come to the same conclusion and put their trust in Jesus.

Presumably Joseph of Arimathea was not at the Council which condemned Jesus, even though he was a member, since the judgement was unanimous. But significantly he was 'waiting for the kingdom of God' (v 51), and as part of that act of waiting he offers his tomb in devotion and respect to Jesus. Did it ever cross his mind that he might have fulfilled a crucial prophecy[4] by this spontaneous act of generosity? Doesn't this illustrate how God in his majesty fulfils his eternal purposes through the unwitting actions of human beings?

The women of the Gospels who ministered to his needs[5] are beyond praise. There they are at the most significant moments: hovering near the cross like a flock of timid birds while Jesus dies and is laid to rest; back there again on Sunday morning, ready to do what was necessary and, with a glorious inevitability, they are the first to greet the risen Jesus. In the meantime, all action stopped for the Sabbath, for exhausted rest before the explosive drama of the new dawn.

While we also 'wait for the kingdom of God' let us make today's jobs an act of worship.

1 I Watts, 1674–1748, 'Alas! and did my Saviour bleed' 2 Heb 10:19–22
3 Acts 10 4 Isa 53:9: 'with a rich man', ESV 5 *See also* Luke 8:2,3

HE IS RISEN!

'We have a hope that is steadfast and certain.'[1] On this Easter morning banish from your mind every fear of death and revel in the joy of your salvation.

LUKE 24:1–12

'For Man, condemned today to lose his dearest, tomorrow himself to pass through the gate of darkness, it remains only to cherish, ere yet the blow falls, the lofty thoughts that ennoble his little day; disdaining the coward terrors of the slave of Fate, to worship at the shrine that his own hands have built.' So wrote the philosopher Bertrand Russell[2] as he contemplated the worldview of twentieth-century rationalism. For him, human beings are the products of time and chance and our only glory is defiance in the face of inevitable death. By contrast, for Jesus God 'is not the God of the dead, but of the living' (20:38), and the angels echo his words: 'He is not here: he has risen!' (v 6). Just think how those words have been taken up in every language and land, turned into simple hymns and great oratorios, gasped by the tortured or shouted in the face of death by the dying and the bereaved; spoken by martyrs from the scaffold and prisoners in death camps. Best of all, they were spoken in the depths of hell when Jesus burst the bonds of death for himself and for us, so that with Paul we may exclaim, 'Where, O death, is your victory? Where, O death, is your sting?'[3]

Which of these views of reality is true? A choice must be made. We must worship either at the shrine of human cleverness or at the empty tomb of Jesus Christ. The first condemns us to the ultimate loneliness of our own self; the second to fullness of joy for evermore.

I love the way Luke speaks of angels in the same breath as material things. We are surrounded by spiritual life as certainly as we are by the electro-magnetic waves which bring television and radio into every corner of the world. Perhaps today you may entertain an angel without knowing it.[4] Be prepared for the unexpected. Jesus is alive!

'Now faith is being sure of what we hope for and certain of what we do not see.' [5] Celebrate our Lord's victory with enthusiasm!

[1] Wendy Churchill, 'Jesus is King', © Springtide/Word Music, 1981 [2] *A Free Man's Worship*, Mosher, 1923 [3] 1 Cor 15:55, quoting Hos 13:14 [4] Heb 13:2 [5] Heb 11:1

WE HAD HOPED...

'And now these three remain: faith, hope and love.'[1] Let your Easter faith lead to renewed hope and acts of love today.

LUKE 24:13–35

There is sheer despair in the simple phrase 'we had hoped' (v 21). Think of your own personal disappointments – a broken romance, a job that didn't materialise, or a sudden bereavement – when a whole structure of excited anticipation was destroyed. All this and more is in that little phrase. But added to their despair was the confusion of the empty tomb and a vision of angels appearing to the women, which was rejected as nonsense by the men (v 11) till one of them met the risen Jesus (vs 33–35) – so it was true after all! What could it all mean?

The risen Jesus had to shake the kaleidoscope of the disciples' knowledge into a new pattern. The events of his life and death were in direct fulfilment of Old Testament writing: the full weight of the sacrificial system, from the Passover ritual to the Levitical sacrifices, the psalms and the prophets are all essential to understanding the atonement. Thus, the writer to the Hebrews could draw on all these sources to explain to wavering Christians how Jesus fulfilled many different aspects of the old covenant revelation. The whole of Scripture bears upon the work of Christ on the cross.

The phrase 'slow of heart' (v 25, NIV) was often used by Jesus to describe the disciples. It is a curious phrase. The problem was not with their thinking but with their believing. (I have a Russian friend who, having been asked to teach a baptismal class, found when he had finished that his knowledge had passed from his head to his heart in a way that changed his life.) So we see that the breaking of bread opened their eyes to the person who had already warmed their hearts. May he burn your heart and open your eyes the next time you share in his Supper.

Have you ever said, 'We had hoped...'? What happened next? Can you be thankful for it?

[1] 1 Cor 13:13

MY BODY ... FOR YOU

'Make no mistake: if he rose at all it was as his body; if the cells' dissolution did not reverse, the molecules re-knit, the amino acids rekindle, the Church will fall.'[1]

LUKE 24:36–53

Luke is very concerned that his readers should understand the very 'physicalness' of the resurrection. The gospel at every stage permeates the material world, concerned with bodies that suffer and need to be healed; with hunger and thirst that need to be satisfied, with human beings who die. So the disciples needed to be reassured that this Jesus was not an apparition or a ghost: the body that was beaten, stabbed and nailed down on beams of wood was the very same body that now stood among them, eating a piece of fish (vs 42,43) and accessible to have its wounds probed by Thomas' sceptical fingers.[2] If death is real, how much more so is the resurrection!

At every stage Jesus wants to remind the disciples of what he had told them about his death and indeed what had long been predicted by prophets. There is a deep mystery in all this. How can history be determined in advance by God and yet be fulfilled by the independent, voluntary acts of responsible human beings?[3] This makes no sense from inside time and space, yet if it were not so God would not be God. We, like the disciples, need to have our minds opened so that we can 'understand the Scriptures' (v 45).

If it was important for the disciples to understand the need for Jesus' death (v 26), they also needed to see Jesus visibly rise from the earth. The Jesus who descended from heaven to the depths of human experience is also the Jesus who has been raised to heaven.[4] There is a man in heaven who bears the scars of his sacrifice – witness that he has made eternal atonement for our sins.[5]

'Let us not mock God with metaphor, analogy, side-stepping transcendence; making of the event a parable, a sign painted in the fading credulity of earlier ages; let us walk through the door.'[6]

---

[1] John Updike, American poet, 1932– , 'Seven stanzas at Easter' [2] John 20:27
[3] Acts 2:23 [4] Phil 2:5–11 [5] Heb 4:14–16; 7:25; 9:24 [6] As note 1

JOHN

John, 'the disciple whom Jesus loved', sets his Gospel in the context of all that has been revealed through Scripture: 'In the beginning was the Word' (1:1). From the start, John makes it clear that he is writing to show his readers that Jesus is the Christ, the Son of God, recording John the Baptist's quotation from Isaiah: 'I am the voice of one calling in the desert, "Make straight the way for the Lord"' (1:23).

The writer is usually thought to have been John, the brother of James. It is generally thought to have been the last Gospel to be written, probably about AD 90. His Gospel covers the life and ministry of Jesus. John emphasises the themes of light and darkness, life and death. He also includes more of Jesus' teaching about the Holy Spirit than any other of the Gospels.

John tells his readers that his Gospel is written, 'that you may believe that Jesus is the Messiah' (20:31). The account of Jesus' life is carefully structured around seven miracles (or signs), usually followed by teaching that shows the inner meaning of what Jesus has done. The teaching also includes the seven 'I am' sayings of Jesus. By the end of the Gospel, the reader must reach a decision about the evidence presented by John and respond to Jesus Christ.

Outline

1 Introduction	1:1-51
2 South and north	2:1 - 4:54
3 A lame man on the Sabbath	5:1-47
4 The five thousand fed	6:1-71
5 At the Feast of Tabernacles	7:1 - 9:41
6 The Good Shepherd	10:1-42
7 The life restorer	11:1-57
8 The last Passover	12:1-50
9 In the Upper Room	13:1-30
10 Getting ready to go	13:31 - 16:33
11 Jesus prays for his own	17:1-26
12 Arrest, trial, crucifixion	18:1 - 19:42
13 Resurrection	20:1 - 21:25

MYSTERIOUS WORD OF GOD

'Tis the Father's pleasure / We should call him Lord / Who from the beginning / Was the mighty Word.'[1]

JOHN 1:1–9

In the silent theatre, lights are dimmed. The opening words of this Gospel echo quietly around us as the curtain rises on a dark stage: 'In the beginning was the Word ... He was with God in the beginning. Through him all things were made.' Slowly, gentle light seeps across the stage. 'In him was life, and that life was the light of all people.' Radiance floods into every corner, spilling off the stage into the auditorium. We shield our eyes from its brilliance. 'The light shines in the darkness, and the darkness has not overcome it.'

Imagine you've never heard these words before, had no prior knowledge of the mysterious Word that is in the beginning. Just as at the start of Genesis God erupts on stage without explanation,[2] so now the Word is presented to us with no preliminaries. Meditate on the Word's existence in time. 'In the beginning' has the sense both of chronology and origin. 'There never was a time when the Word was not. There never was a thing which did not depend on Him for its very existence.'[3] Meditate on the Word in relationship: the phrases 'with God' and 'in the beginning with God' describe the closest possible intimacy of God and Word. And meditate on the Word's identity: 'the Word was God.' The claim is that this so far unidentified Word is divine.

And as a spotlight falls on a shabby, unremarkable figure who simply gestures towards the flooding radiance (vs 6,7), meditate also on the Word's generous embrace. No one is excluded from this communication. John the Baptist points to the Word 'so that all might believe through him' (v 7). This Word is 'the light of all people' (v 4), the light 'which gives light to everyone' (v 9).

'We may well wonder how the universal dimensions of the hope of the gospel ... have so often suffered eclipse within the church.'[4] Lord, teach us to love the world with your all-embracing heart.

---

[1] CM Noel, 1817–77, 'At the Name of Jesus' [2] Gen 1:1 [3] L Morris, *The Gospel according to John*, Eerdmans, 1971, p73 [4] David Smith, *Moving towards Emmaus*, SPCK, 2007, p69

GRACE AND TRUTH

Lord, we worship you as we consider your incarnation: 'Our God contracted to a span, Incomprehensibly made Man.'[1]

JOHN 1:10-18

In a powerful sermon on Christmas morning in 2006, Tom Wright, the Bishop of Durham, focused his congregation's attention on a theme not often explored in relation to the Word become flesh.[2] He opened up the implications of John's significantly repeated description of Jesus the incarnate Word. Jesus is 'full of grace and truth' and he brings these gifts with him (vs 14,17). The roots of this thought, as of so many other aspects of this Prologue, lie in the Old Testament. In this case it is Psalm 85, a prayer for restoration which becomes a hopeful vision of God's peace and salvation, springing out of the seemingly impossible coming together of grace, or mercy, with truth.[3]

Only God himself can bring about this fusion. I have a vivid memory of David Porter, director of the Evangelical Contribution on Northern Ireland (now the Centre for Contemporary Christianity in Ireland) helping a group of us to experience the tensions of the Northern Ireland peace process by 'becoming' the values of Psalm 85:10 - grace and truth, justice and peace. We all urged the priority of 'our' values and were shocked at the human impossibility of these ever coming together in harmony. 'Our world has tried … to get truth without grace; and the church has been in danger for a long time of offering grace without truth.'[4]

As we continue to explore John's unfolding story of Jesus we will see how he uniquely holds mercy and truth together in creative and astounding tension. As he does so we witness God himself in action, Jesus revealing the essence, the inmost heart of God (v 18), Jesus empowering us who receive him also to hold grace and truth together in our daily lives and dealings with each other (vs 12,16).

Today, meditate prayerfully on how 'we can be people, we can become communities, in whom God's grace generates and sustains a human integrity, a wholeness and holiness of character.'[5]

[1] C Wesley, 1707–88 [2] www.ntwrightpage.com/sermons/Christmas06.htm [3] Ps 85:10 (AV) [4] Wright, sermon, p4 [5] Wright, sermon, p5

WHO ARE YOU?

'You, O LORD, know me; You see me and test me – my heart is with you.'[1]

JOHN 1:19–34

John's spotlight moves from Jesus, God's perfect communication, to John the Baptist, sent from God to offer evidence of Jesus (vs 7,19). Our text today opens up the nature of John's evidence – both negative (vs 19-27) and positive (vs 29-34), and paints a partial portrait of one of the most intriguing people in the Bible. In this Gospel, John bursts on the scene, like the Word himself, without preliminaries. We are told nothing of his remarkable birth, unconventional desert life and the fierce preaching recorded in the Synoptic Gospels.[2]

John, like the Jesus of whom he gives evidence, faces searching and hostile questions about his identity from those who seek to define and categorise in order to control. If John believed himself to be the fulfilment of prophecies in Malachi or Deuteronomy,[3] then the Pharisees wanted to know. What were John's credentials for his strange ministry (v 25)? John's reply is passionately negative – look at the verbs heaped up in verses 20 and 21: No, I'm not the Messiah, not Elijah, not Moses. My identity only has significance as it relates to another's identity – one that you're not even aware of yet (v 26).

In contrast to John's humble self-identification is the confident assurance with which he identifies Jesus. In this Gospel John's recognition is not a matter of family ties or familiarity, but of revelation – the gift of God – as he witnesses the coming of the Spirit on Jesus at his baptism (vs 32,33). This was surely an epiphany that confirmed John's understanding of himself and his calling, and validated all the irregularity that so upset the religious establishment. David Smith comments on the Emmaus epiphany that 'when religion ceases to be merely conventional … it produces forms of behaviour that are bound to appear irrational and reckless to normal, well-adjusted people.'[4]

For reflection: 'Jesus confers on John his true significance. No [person] is what he himself thinks he is. He is only what Jesus knows him to be.'[5]

[1] Jer 12:3, NRSV [2] Luke 1,3 [3] Deut 18:15–18; Mal 4:5 [4] Smith, *Emmaus*, p86
[5] Morris, *John*, pp135,136

FREE TO FOLLOW

Lord, thank you for your continuing invitations to look at you, listen to you and stay in your company.

JOHN 1:35–42

In his commentary, Leon Morris makes the intriguing suggestion that the opening section of John's Gospel reflects the creation narrative in Genesis, not only by its 'In the beginning' language but also through the narrative structure itself. The repeated phrase 'The next day...' (vs 29,35,43) unobtrusively reminds us of an unfolding week, each day of which brings events that are significant in their newness.[1]

The third day of this momentous week is characterised by a surprising restfulness, the antithesis of the Pharisees' anxious desire to control (vs 24,25). What is nothing less than the beginning of the church starts with a successful leader stepping back so that Andrew and his companion are free to transfer their allegiance to Jesus. I wonder how John felt as he watched these two men walk away from him. How different the history of the church would be if its leaders followed the example of John the Baptist, secure in his identity and calling, consistently pointing to Jesus, free of a competitive spirit.

There's an ease too about the first encounter between Jesus and Andrew and his companion. No checking of their credentials, no pressure to sign on, simply an open invitation to explore further (v 38). Again and again over the next three years Jesus will probe people with questions like this, refusing to manipulate or pressurise them to respond to him.[2] The men's oblique reply (v 38) might hint at shyness on their part. Though it's already four in the afternoon (v 39), Jesus generously makes himself and his lodgings available to them. Perhaps they stayed the night. Whatever was said during that long conversation transformed Andrew into a willing witness in the context where witness is often hardest: our own family. His brother would be the first of several people Andrew brought to Jesus (6:8,9; 12:21,22).

'Embedded at the very centre of the Christian story is the principle that genuine faith cannot be compelled.'[3]

[1] Morris, *John*, pp129,130 [2] Matt 20:32; Mark 10:36 [3] Smith, *Emmaus*, p60

COME AND SEE

'Will you come and follow me / if I but call your name? / Will you go where you don't know / and never be the same?'[1]

JOHN 1:43–51

The fourth day of this significant week makes it clear that there is no one way in which Jesus brings together the core group of his followers. Perhaps one of the most problematic aspects of the church is its tendency to standardise the entry process into the community of faith, instead of recognising and celebrating the different and surprising ways in which God is at work in different people.

The pace of John's narrative speeds up. For reasons that are not clear, Jesus is on the move northwards to Galilee (v 43) where John has been baptising in the Jordan valley (1:28). He now takes the initiative to recruit Philip, calling him in the same terms ('Follow me') that the synoptic writers use for Jesus calling other disciples.[2] The picture that John paints of Philip in the rest of the Gospel is of a rather slow-thinking and slow-acting man (6:5,7; 12:20–22; 14:8), a contrast to the dynamic Peter. In matters of faith, though, Philip is impressively clear. He has made connections that only openness to God's Spirit can make. The Torah texts and the prophecies that he has chewed over for so long now have a face, a face from here in Galilee itself (v 45)! Faced with his friend's scepticism, Philip acts with uncomplicated wisdom. No anger, no counter-arguments, just Jesus' own approach of 'Come and see' (vs 39,46).

Tom Wright suggests that John invites us to enjoy a moment of humour in the brief exchange between the enthusiastic Philip and the rather Eeyore-like Nathanael, whose home town of Cana (21:2) was Nazareth's arch rival (vs 45,46)![3] Can we imagine gentle laughter in Jesus' voice as he responds to Nathanael's astounded worship (v 50)? And do we hear the contrasting solemnity of his closing promise and his use of the name, 'Son of Man' (v 51)?[4]

What aspects of Jesus have you discovered during the past year that you would want to invite others to come and see?

[1] John Bell, Graham Maule, Wild Goose Resource Group, Iona Community
[2] Matt 9:9; Mark 1:17 [3] Tom Wright, *John*, SPCK, 2002, p19 [4] *Cf* Ps 8:4, AV; Dan 7:13, AV

WHATEVER HE TELLS YOU...

'Lord, your Word unfailingly calls us to follow you, to be ready for you to change us. Deal with our fear of change, our dread of obedience, we pray.'[1]

JOHN 2:1–11

'My pastoral experience has been that Bible studies in the evangelical mode haven't produced much Bible living.' This was the reply that came from a well-known writer and pastor when I wrote to ask him how he had gone about helping people engage with Scripture. 'After a few years of trying to train my congregation in inductive Bible study methods, I relaxed and shifted ground to prayer/conversation groups over the text.'

Why is it that Bible study and Bible knowledge so rarely result in God-shaped living? There are no simple answers, but this story may help. The least important people at that wedding reception in Cana – the kitchen staff – take seriously their instructions from Jesus' mother to 'do whatever he tells you.' Our familiarity with the story makes us forget to stand in the shoes of the servants as they laboured to fill the huge water jars. Did they make any connection between Jesus' order and the catastrophe of the wine running out? And imagine that moment when they again obey Jesus and dip a goblet into what they know was, seconds ago, ordinary water from the well. Imagine their thoughts as they take the sample (untested by them!) to the steward (v 9). Did they fear their jobs were on the line? Or did some conviction of Jesus' absolute reliability hold them steady? The servants' responsive actions are a model of the kind of following that this Gospel urges us to imitate. So is the instinctive and immediate turning of Jesus' mother to her son in the face of crisis (v 3). Eugene Peterson insists that 'the Bible, all of it, is liveable; it is the text for living our lives ... We are given this book so that we can imaginatively and believingly enter the world of the text and follow Jesus.'[2]

The first sign by which Jesus 'revealed his glory' (v 11) is one of thoughtful kindness. Meditate on this in the light of Galatians 5:22,23. Be alert to opportunities to follow him today.

[1] Lesslie Newbigin, *The Light Has Come*, Eerdmans, 1982, p25 [2] E Peterson, *Eat This Book: the Art of Spiritual Reading*, Hodder & Stoughton, 2006, pp18,69

ANGRY WORD

'May the light of God illumine the heart of my soul. May the flame of Christ kindle me to love. May the fire of the Spirit free me to live.'[1]

JOHN 2:12–25

If, during Jesus' short ministry, he engaged in only one 'cleansing' of the Jerusalem Temple, then we must accept that John has placed the event at a quite different point from that recorded by the other Gospel writers. Their accounts locate this encounter in the last week of Jesus' life, not at the start of his ministry.[2] So why might John choose to present this material near the opening of his Gospel? Perhaps it was in order to reinforce his opening theme of the light that shines in the darkness, which cannot overcome it (1:5).

This darkness has crept insidiously into the very place where people should rightly hope to be drawn into light and life, the welcoming Father's 'house of prayer for all nations'[3] (cf v 16). The racket of commercial activities that so angered Jesus was particularly focused in the court of the Gentiles, the one place in the Jerusalem Temple where non-Jews, 'outsiders', people like the Ethiopian eunuch,[4] might have access. Both Jesus' outraged sweeping away of everything that made the Temple systems workable, and his provocative challenge (v 19) point again to something absolutely new, as different from the long-established religious systems and structures as wine is different from water (vs 20,21).

A scene like this invites us to enter into it and meditate on where we might find ourselves, and in what state of mind. Are we among those who watch anxiously as our untried leader makes his whip and turns on what we'd long understood to be perfectly legitimate activities (vs 17,22)? Or among those for whom organised religion is a vital commercial opportunity (vs 14–16)? Or an arena in which to exercise power over others (v 18)? Or might we be among those who look on in astounded joy as Jesus acts in anger?

Lord Jesus, Word of life, Light of the world, give us courage and discernment in this coming year to identify and act with you in what makes you angry.

1 JP Newell, *Celtic Benediction*, Canterbury, 2000, p5 2 Matt 21; Mark 11; Luke 19 3 Isa 56:7 4 Acts 8:27

THE LIMITS OF RELIGION

'No condemnation now I dread! Jesus, and all in him, is mine.'[1] Thank God for the gift of his love.

JOHN 3:1–21

Nicodemus is a religious expert, but John describes him first simply as a man who comes to Jesus and addresses him in the terms he already knows: Rabbi, Teacher. We can but guess what was in his mind. Why did Jesus start talking about the new birth before Nicodemus had even asked a question? The 'for' in verse 16 signals that the evangelist is about to explain what has just happened. Nicodemus observed that Jesus 'has come from God' (v 2). One implied question is, for what purpose is he sent? Verse 16 is the resounding answer. He is sent because God loved not only the Jewish people, but the world. He is not sent to expound or extend the laws that make the Jews a holy people, and so to strengthen the difference between those who are 'in' and those who are 'out', but to offer life to all.

The implied alternative is that God sent Jesus into the world to teach the Law, and therefore to condemn.[2] Teaching – whether of doctrine or of Law – tends to produce two responses in those who accept it. Some think they are following it, resulting in self-righteousness and condemnation of others. Some recognise that they don't or can't follow it, and so feel condemned. The Qur'an pictures prophets as people sent to proclaim God's sovereignty and teach his laws. Their teaching divides the hearers into unbelievers, who are destroyed, and believers, who are preserved. Muslims, who see themselves as those who have accepted the prophetic messengers, often either feel condemned because they don't keep the laws or think themselves righteous and condemn others. The Qur'an, like John 3:18–20, recognises that many hearts are locked against God,[3] but attempts to unlock them by exhortations, promises and threats. Today's reading is good news for people of every religion: we cannot keep God's laws, but we can be born again. The love of God in Christ unlocks closed hearts.

Tell someone today about how God's love in Christ unlocked your heart.

[1] Charles Wesley, 1707–88, 'And can it be' [2] Greek *krino* means either 'judge' or 'condemn' (3:17) [3] Surah 47:24; 63:3; *cf* 7:100; 17:46

THE VIEW FROM 'ABOVE'

'Since, then, you have been raised with Christ, set your heart on things above, where Christ is seated at the right hand of God.'¹

JOHN 3:22–36

Yesterday we saw the questions being asked by one Jewish leader. Today's reading introduces another debate, on ritual cleanliness. The answer, as always in John's Gospel, is found in Jesus.

John the Baptist's disciples are questioned by a Jew – perhaps a representative of a particular group. We do not know what they discussed, but we do know that, for first-century Jews, the question of how to be sufficiently clean to worship God was as important as it is for twenty-first-century Hindus and Muslims. John's baptism would have been seen as a particular kind of ritual washing, signifying repentance and a new beginning. His disciples would, perhaps, have told the Jew about the need for such a new beginning. Certainly, they do not ask John about whatever they have discussed with him. Instead, they raise a related issue: who should baptise? Questions about leadership and authority are common to all religions!

John the Baptist's role in John's Gospel is to witness to Jesus. His response to his disciples shows him doing the work for which God sent him – pointing to Jesus and not to himself. What matters is not who does a particular job, but that each accepts what God has given. It is the view 'from above'² that matters.

Questions of ritual and leadership usually focus on human activity: they view religion 'from below'. Every religion recognises that the goal is 'above', but, unless someone comes 'from above', we are likely to get stuck on 'from below' questions. Verses 31–36 show us an open heaven, from which, through the Son, we receive all that we need and to which we can belong for ever if we accept him. If we stay focused on 'below' and reject the Son, all our attempts at cleanliness miss what really matters and leave us under the wrath of God.

Where do you see people focusing on questions of ritual and leadership 'from below'? How can you help them towards a heavenly perspective?

1 Col 3:1 2 The Greek word translated 'above' here is translated 'again' in 3:3,7

SCANDALOUS ENCOUNTER

God knows all I have ever done, but he still wants me. Hallelujah!

The heroine of John 4 should have been excluded from knowing Jesus on three counts: she was a woman; she was a Samaritan; she was 'bad'. In a society in which both marriage and divorce happened by male prerogative, she had been rejected five times, and had now been taken in by someone who was using her illegitimately. In such situations, then as now, the woman gets the blame. She brings shame on her family, and is avoided as someone who is wicked or brings bad luck. No religious person associates with someone like her. They must demonstrate society's condemnation of deviant behaviour.

Whatever the questions on the woman's lips, the longing of her heart is surely to find acceptance. Jesus' willingness to spend time with her is one of the most graphic illustrations of 3:16-21 - the work for which God sent Jesus was not condemnation but new life. As the woman accepts the Light that shows up her darkest places, she not only discovers who that Light is but also finds a way back into her community. Like that other rejected foreigner, the mother of Ishmael, it is at a well that she meets God, 'the Living One who sees me'.[1]

As with Nicodemus, Jesus responds to her first speech with a provocative offer of new life (v 10; cf 3:3). Like Nicodemus, the woman first understands him in material terms, and asks 'How?' (v 11; cf 3:9). Unlike Nicodemus, she responds to further explanation by accepting Jesus' offer, even though she probably doesn't understand it. Jesus takes her seriously, and it is not to the religious leader but to this woman that he first, in this Gospel, says 'I am' (v 26).

Ask God to lead you into conversation with someone you would not normally associate with, who feels condemned by their own community. Take Jesus as your example for relating with them.

---

[1] Gen 16:13,14 (see TNIV footnote)

JESUS' MOTIVATION

Lord, give me a glimpse of your heart today!

JOHN 4:27–42

The disciples have been thinking about dinner. Jesus has been fulfilling the purpose of his life. The disciples see their rabbi breaking the taboos. Jesus sees a condemned woman who needs the salvation he has come to bring.

What about the woman? She slips away, leaving behind her water pot, forgetting the water that she came for. The telling of 'everything I've ever done' (v 29) is no longer shamefully avoided, but proclaimed with excitement as she asks who this man might be. What a transformation! Jesus has dealt with her shameful past in a way that brings not condemnation but life! Jesus is just as excited as the woman. This is his meat and drink (v 32). This is why he came. Here, after all the questions and half-faith at the centre of Jewish worship, is someone thirsty for the living waters, who is on her way to tell a community ripe for harvest about him. Can't the disciples see?

And what about the Samaritans? It is among these most unlikely people that we see the first group movement to faith in John's Gospel. John tells us that many believed in response to his Jerusalem healings, but follows this with the comment that Jesus did not commit himself to them.[1] The faith of these Jerusalem believers was, it seems, a shallow belief based only on miracles – like the faith that is criticised in tomorrow's reading. In contrast, he trusts his true identity to the woman at the well, and the Samaritan villagers recognise 'the Saviour of the world' (v 42). John 4:1-45 is the practical outworking of the theology of chapter 3: God's purpose of saving the world is seen first in Jesus' mission to the very people with whom his own natural ethnic group might have had the greatest hostility.

What is the work for which God has sent you? When was it last more important to you than your dinner?!

[1] John 2:23,24

SIGN OF LIFE

Lord, I want to honour you in all that I do and say and think!

JOHN 4:43-54

Jesus returns to the scene of his first sign, and we meet another man who, having heard about him, comes to him. He is described as a 'royal official' (v 46), which probably means that he worked in Herod's court. While Nicodemus was from the religious hierarchy, this man worked in a place of political power. His questions are not about law or ritual; and the longing of his heart is very straightforward: he wants his son to live. Jesus pushes him on whether he will truly believe, but he sees only the need of his son and the hope that there is in Jesus.

This passage seems so simple after the theological discussions so far, yet it summarises them all. The message of John 3 and 4 is simple: we are all - religious leader or social outcast, prophet's disciple or state official - in danger of eternal death, but God has sent Jesus so that we can have eternal life instead. Why has he done it? Because he loves us! How can we have it? By coming and asking.

There is a darker side here, however. In verse 45, the evangelist tells us that Jesus received a welcome in Galilee, apparently based on his Jerusalem miracles - but he has just warned us that a prophet is not honoured in his home area. What does this apparent contradiction mean? The clues are in John 2:23-25 and 4:48. A faith that is based entirely on seeing and desiring miracles is inadequate. It does not honour Jesus, and to a person who has only such a faith Jesus will not show his true identity. The mention of the first sign in verse 46 is a reminder of Jesus' true purpose. Inadequate faith focuses on the signs, and does not see what they are pointing to. The official's belief in Jesus' word reminds us that Jesus is the Word,[1] and suggests that his faith reaches beyond the signs to the Christ himself.

Which of your loved ones is in danger of eternal death? Come to the Lord of Life today and ask him to save them.

[1] Cf John 1:1

MISSING THE MIRACLE

'There is a balm in Gilead that makes the wounded whole. There is a balm in Gilead that heals the sin-sick soul.'[1]

JOHN 5:1–15

Some years ago I visited a steaming hot pool not far from Jerusalem where arthritic and infirm people soothed their joints joyfully under the warm, bubbling, sulphur spring. So I can picture the people at Bethesda, with all kinds of ailments and disabilities, hoping that the curative waters might bring them healing (even if verse 4, which attributes the stirring of the waters to an angel, was added later). But there was frustration there as well as joy. The man paralysed for 38 years was both isolated and defeated by his infirmity. So the question from Jesus, 'Do you want to get well?' (v 6) must have sounded odd to him.

God often challenges us about what we really want. Do we want to live differently? Do we want to move forward in faith? Staying as we are, even when dissatisfied with life, suggests we don't know what we want, or we're not prepared to face the challenge of change. Sometimes, like this man, we do know what we want, but we are looking for it in the wrong place. He found, as we find also, that it is only when we act in faith and obedience to Christ that miracles happen and new life opens up.

In this passage, there were also those who wanted things to stay just the same. They were the religious leaders. Ironically they were furthest of all from faith and obedience and so absorbed in legalism and the trappings of religion that they couldn't even see what had happened. The crowds saw someone healed after 38 years. The legalists saw someone carrying a mat on the Sabbath. How tragic to be so concerned to defend religion that they missed the miracle!

God is doing small miracles every day in people around us. With each miracle comes the challenge of verse 14: to let go of the sins that hold us back, and enjoy freedom.

Lord, give me the right mentality so that I can understand what you ask and work with you; and give me the faith to see you at work.

[1] African-American spiritual

EQUAL WITH GOD

'For God was pleased to have all his fullness dwell in him, and through him to reconcile to himself all things.'[1]

JOHN 5:16–30

We tend to forget that, for much of his ministry, Jesus was facing people who wanted to kill him. The Jewish leaders now identify Jesus as a problem. He has overturned the Temple traders and stories of his healings race round Jerusalem. He undermines their control of the Sabbath, winning popularity with the people. So the leaders want to get rid of him. In fact they seem prepared to murder to support their insistence on law – a slight inconsistency perhaps!

It is what Jesus says about God which enrages them most. He claims a special relationship with God, even calling himself the Son of God. He makes bold parallels between God's work and his, between God's power and his, disclosing something of the intimacy between the Father and the Son. It is impossible for the leaders to miss the implication. This man is assuming some sort of equality with God. This has to be blasphemy – and of course to claim equality with God is blasphemy. Whenever people have elevated themselves in this way the consequences have been terrible. Pharoahs, kings and cult leaders down the ages who promoted themselves to a place of divinity have assumed absolute authority over the lives of others. The results have been tyranny and death. Some of us have experiences of people assuming the place of God in our lives, and we know how destructive this is.

But not so with Jesus. For, since he is equal with God he knows the very heart of the Father and it is a heart of truth and love. Jesus does not bring bondage and destruction, but freedom from condemnation to those who receive him (vs 24–26). His critics were offered eternal life by the Son of God himself, yet pride and prejudice would not let them accept his offer. Let us ask God's Spirit to keep our hearts always open, and ready to hear.

Lord, we thank you that you show us the heart of the Father, and you draw us closer to his love.

[1] Col 1:19,20

SEARCHING THE SCRIPTURES

'Beyond the sacred page I seek Thee, Lord; My spirit longs for Thee, O living Word.'[1]

JOHN 5:31–47

There is the feel of a courtroom in this passage. Jesus calls three witnesses to give evidence about his true identity. First, he cites John the Baptist. John had baptised Jesus and heard the voice from heaven saying, 'This is my beloved Son.'[2] Next, Jesus cites the work he is doing. Although not yet complete, the teaching and miracles already give signs of who Jesus is. Third, he cites the testimony of the Scriptures: that he is the one of whom Moses wrote, and the prophets prophesied. The whole of God's revelation points to the truth of Jesus as the Christ.

Yet Jesus already knows his hearers will not be convinced. To recognise the truth of these testimonies, they need to have hearts that are open to the love of God, and this is what is lacking. Their hearts are closed. The irony here is that Jesus is actually talking to professional 'Scripture searchers' - people who teach others what the Bible says. They revere Moses as the lawgiver, yet it will be Moses who will ultimately condemn them for their unbelief (vs 45,46). For all their knowledge, they stay in ignorance, lacking the humility and love to discern the truth about Jesus as God's Word incarnate.

The problem with these religious leaders was not that they ignored Scripture, but that effectively, they worshipped it. They loved the legal niceties, the arguments, the genealogies - but somehow they missed the point of searching the Scriptures, which is to encounter the living God (vs 39,40). I remember once being at a fiery debate over New Testament doctrine. People relished the arguments, with each side claiming to be more orthodox than the other. It was stimulating, but I came away wondering if Jesus hadn't somehow got lost in abstractions. Even orthodoxy is empty without him. When we don't let the Bible lead us to God, we can turn even the Scriptures into an idol.

Lord, let my love of your Word never surpass my love for you.

1 Mary Lathbury, 1841–1913, 'Break Thou the bread of life' 2 Matt 3:17, AV

HUNGRY FOR ACTION

'Bless Thou the Bread of Life to me, to me; as Thou didst bless the loaves by Galilee.'[1] Show me, Lord, how your provision reaches into every area of life.

JOHN 6:1–15

We've probably all experienced visitors arriving unexpectedly so we are caught unprepared, asking: 'What can we give them to eat?' Jesus puts that question to his disciples. He has two different answers. Philip is entirely realistic – we don't have the money to feed them! Andrew is entirely unrealistic – can we do anything with this lad's lunch?

In fact, five small loaves and two small fish turn out to be the perfectly sufficient ingredients for a miracle. The whole crowd is fed and the disciples have a basketful of leftovers each to distribute to hungry people on the way home. It is clear that normal human experiences of what is realistic often have to be revised when God is at work. How many times have Christians said, 'Eight months' wages wouldn't be enough to see us through this crisis!', only to find that a miracle happens? God changes the circumstances, or touches the hearts of people so they give, and the crisis evaporates.

Nevertheless, 5,000 men is a huge crowd, and it is interesting to know why so many were there. John implies that they came running after Jesus because they saw him as a political as well as a spiritual figure. This could have been a potential uprising against the Roman occupiers. Verse 15 is significant – Jesus knew the crowd intended to make him king by force, so he slipped away. If the crowds wanted political action, they got Jesus wrong. But if we just 'spiritualise' his teachings we can get him wrong also – eliminating the political and social relevance from who he is. To call Jesus the 'Christ' is to recognise that his Word reaches all of life. We must learn from him about power, rule, justice and authority. Christ is the King and challenges every dominion of this world, yet he still feeds the hungry.

Have you shut Jesus out of political and economic areas? Consider: 'This too is politics: "let them have food." Feeding and healing are Jesus' concerns, not a Herodian rebellion.'[2]

[1] Lathbury, 'Break Thou the bread of life' [2] Alan Storkey, *Jesus and Politics*, Baker, 2005, p88

FEAR AND THE UNKNOWN

'Eternal Father, strong to save, whose arm hath bound the restless wave
... From rock and tempest, fire and foe, protect us wheresoe'er we go.'[1]

JOHN 6:16–24

Sometimes we experience situations that are full of confusion. The situations in today's passage are like that. The disciples are expecting to go to Capernaum, but by nightfall Jesus has not joined them, so they sail off without him. The crowds are also confused about where Jesus is and why he is not in the boat, and they seem determined to track him down (v 24).The disciples then face a dreadful storm and the boat threatens to capsize. When a figure walks towards them on the water their confusion turns to fear and panic. It is only when someone recognises it is Jesus and he is hauled on board that the confusion and anxiety dissipate and relief spreads among them. Before they know it, they are safely at the other side and all is well.

A storm at sea is not something to take lightly, and on the Sea of Galilee calm can change quite rapidly into raging tempest. Yet the storm itself didn't terrify the disciples. They were afraid, but they had been through this before. It was the unknown which terrified them - the startling sight of someone walking across the sea. This they had not been through before.

It is often like this with us. We can more easily face the things we know and understand, even when they are bad, than those things which seem random or unpredictable. When we have no idea what is happening, or what might come next we can be very afraid. The reassuring thing is that God understands what is happening and can help us to confront our fear. The irony in the passage is that what the disciples feared most was what brought them help and rescue. It can be so with us. We can find that confronting our fear with Jesus might not remove us from problems or dangers, but it does give us the ability to bear the storm.

What are your main fears right now? What are your chief fears for the future? Confront them honestly, and bring them to God.

[1] William Whiting, 1825–78, altd

BREAD OF LIFE

'Why spend money on what is not bread ...?'[1]

Bread is very significant in our relationship with God. It is one of the few things we ask for specifically in the Lord's Prayer. God's provision of bread – manna – in the wilderness is deeply etched in the collective memory of the Jewish people. When Jesus talks about bread, it stands for what is most central to the needs of human beings – spiritual as well as bodily.

Yet the people following Jesus are transfixed on its ordinary meaning. They are beginning to see him as someone who can provide for their material needs, so the conversation he has with them is both challenging and difficult. In order for them to believe in Jesus they demand more miraculous bread as a sign from God. Instead, Jesus offers himself as the bread of life, telling them that faith in him will sustain them whatever the circumstances, even through death. This challenge is for us too. We can so easily see faith in Christ as conferring benefits on us – giving us some guarantee that our needs will be met, and that 'God will provide' – and indeed God does, but the provisions we are given are not always what we ask for. We may ask for material well-being, but God may instead enlarge our capacity to manage with less. We may ask for better health, but receive more patience to bear affliction. We may ask for problems to be resolved, but be given greater trust and perseverance. Accepting Jesus as the bread of life does not mean that we will always eat cake!

Jesus does give us that wonderful assurance that whoever comes to him will never be turned away, for the relationship on offer is one that lasts a lifetime, and beyond. Whatever our circumstances, our security is anchored in the will of God – that we will be part of the resurrection and eternal life which Christ has come to bring us.

A hard question: do the blessings you receive draw you closer to God or tempt you to find your security elsewhere?

[1] Isa 55:2a

WHEN FOLLOWING IS HARD

'When he had given thanks, he broke it and said, "This is my body, which is for you; do this in remembrance of me."'[1]

JOHN 6:41–71

Jesus did not always make it easy for his hearers to understand. Words about eating flesh and drinking blood had some significance for first-century Jews, but this was linked with animal sacrifice. Christians understand his words here to be Jesus initiating the practice of communion, where as the body of Christ we symbolically receive the body of Christ together. Yet even here, Christian traditions differ about whether they see it as predominantly sacramental (Jesus giving life to those participating through the wine and bread) or commemorative (an act of remembrance).

The people listening to Jesus did not have two thousand years of Christian history to try to sort this out. Struggling with what it meant to 'feed' on Christ was too much for some of them. John tells us that many 'turned back and no longer followed him' (v 66). It isn't clear what the problems were. Perhaps they were intellectual ones; people couldn't grasp his teaching – drinking blood was forbidden to God's people.[2] Perhaps they were problems of belief; they found it hard to trust that Christ's words really were 'spirit and life' (v 63) and that by feeding on him they would live for ever. Perhaps they realised he was not the sort of leader they wanted, but someone who made too many demands on their lives.

It is encouraging that the disciples reacted differently: 'To whom shall we go? You have the words of eternal life' (v 68). This is no glib statement, but one which takes seriously the choice that has to be made. It is a choice which many of us face at difficult times of our lives.

Begin to pray for those people you know who have 'turned back' from the Christian faith, and make prayer for them a commitment this week.

[1] 1 Cor 11:24 [2] Lev 7:26,27

TIME TO CONFRONT?

'Judge nothing before the appointed time; wait till the Lord comes. He will bring to light what is hidden in darkness and will expose the motives of people's hearts.'[1]

JOHN 7:1–24

Sometimes family members don't want each other to know their plans, but this level of secrecy from Jesus seems extreme. They want him to go to the Feast of Tabernacles and make a public display of his miracles, but clearly he doesn't fully trust them. This is not surprising when John tells us that they don't actually believe in him. Instead, Jesus goes to the feast incognito, so he can hear what people are saying. When, halfway through the feast, he begins to teach publicly at the Temple courts, he can speak directly into the situation that he has witnessed. Listening and observing are even more crucial for us than they were for Jesus. How often we need to learn to listen and absorb what people are saying and thinking, before we speak ourselves!

It is clear to Jesus that he needs to confront the leaders with their hypocrisy and their evil intentions, even though the crowd won't understand (v 20), so he exposes their inconsistencies. The leaders maintain the Mosaic Law, which forbids killing, but they intend to kill Jesus. They fulfil the Law by circumcising on the Sabbath, yet deny Jesus the right to heal on the Sabbath. The implications are clear – they need some self-critical discernment (v 24). It's a very different outcome from what his brothers wanted. Rather than entertain the crowds and impress the leaders with his miraculous powers, Jesus brings them tough rebukes from God and challenges them about their shallow insincerity. Confronting what lies below the surface is never easy, especially when people work hard to keep things hidden. It is the job of the Holy Spirit. When, sometimes, he urges us to confront others we must respond, but first we must seek discernment, pray for insight, and allow God to confront us also.

How able are you to address the things that lie below the surface in your family or work relationships? Pray now for wisdom and courage to know the way ahead.

[1] 1 Cor 4:5

A PEOPLE DIVIDED

'No one ever spoke the way this man does.'[1]

JOHN 7:25–52

I am always surprised how differently people react to the same person, or the same event. There is so much in our background or our mentality which predisposes us to respond to others in certain ways. In this passage the differences are fuelled by the confusion among the crowd. They can't understand what Jesus means about where he has come from or where he is going (vs 27,28,35,36), so the debate heats up and two quite definite responses emerge.

The first is the Pharisaic response. They evaluate Jesus externally, holding him up against their interpretation of the prophets, but their own knowledge is faulty and they see him only as a Galilean, and not as one born in Bethlehem (vs 41,52). So, on the basis of flimsy information, and pride in their own knowledge, they reject Jesus as the Messiah. The second is the people's response. They evaluate Jesus experientially, holding the prophecies up against their experience of him. They see the miracles, hear the teaching, glimpse the presence of the Holy Spirit (vs 39,40), and the offer of 'living water' – and they get him right: 'He is the Messiah' (v 41).

People have been divided about Jesus throughout history. In every place where the gospel has been preached there have been those who have rejected Christ and those who have accepted him. Our task is not to probe why, but to continue to believe, ourselves, and witness to the truth. When we do, we will often court the same response that the crowd got from the self-important leaders. Scorn, derision and ridicule are usually the weapons used by people who have not managed to impose their views any other way (v 47)! Such negative responses do not deter Jesus, nor should they deter us. For he promises us power from the Spirit to offer life in his name, to all who will receive.

Lord, help us through our lives to give other people the experience of Christ's power and love. May our actions help others to glorify our Father in heaven.[2]

[1] John 7:46 [2] Matt 5:16

GUILTY, NOT CONDEMNED!

'No condemnation now I dread; Jesus, and all in him, is mine! '[1]

JOHN 7:53 – 8:11

The woman taken in adultery was to be a test case for Jesus. His critics must have anticipated that he would not be very keen on her being stoned, but to order her release they required him to contradict the Law given by Moses, that an adulterer must be put to death.[2] It is interesting, however, that only the woman is brought to Jesus. Adultery involves two people, and the Law of Moses made it clear that both of them should be punished equally. If the woman was actually caught committing adultery, the man must also have been identified, yet he is not brought to be judged. The partiality of the Pharisees and teachers of the Law is very evident.

In refusing to debate with them, or even to break off from writing on the ground, Jesus refuses to entertain their hypocrisy. His challenge that those without sin should cast the first stone not only silences the critics and frees the woman, but it echoes down through time as an indictment of all of us. None of us is free from sin, yet how much outrage, throughout history, has been expressed at the sins of others! It is interesting that the crowd melts away, even without a glance from Jesus. The power of his words is sufficient, especially apparently for the older ones who leave first. When he finally speaks to the woman, her sin is not condoned, and Jesus asks her to leave it behind. But he refuses to condemn her, because no one now brings any charge.

There is a connection between our release of someone's guilt, and God's forgiveness. When we offer someone mercy, we are echoing what the grace of God does through Jesus. And when the righteous Christ intervenes on our behalf, and says 'neither do I condemn', he brings us the most liberating sentence in the world.

In which specific areas of your life are you most conscious of having received God's forgiveness? Are there areas where you still need to know release? Pray for this now.

[1] Charles Wesley, 1707–88, 'And can it be' [2] Lev 20:10

WALKING IN GOD'S LIGHT

Thank you, Father, for the light of Christ, shining in the darkness of the world. Help me truly to 'follow him' and experience 'the light of life'.

JOHN 8:12–30

The opening verse of this section implies that Jesus here resumes the teaching begun during the Feast of Tabernacles (7:2). If this is so, his stupendous claim to be 'the light of the world' connects with symbolic actions during the festival in which Israel's experience of being led through the wilderness by the provision of supernatural light[1] was recalled by the lighting of four golden candlesticks. It is said that the light thus created shone across the night sky of Jerusalem. Perhaps the nearest equivalent we can find would be a brilliant firework display at the end of a modern festival.

As a wonderful communicator, therefore, Jesus uses the impact of this event to claim that the light he brings, in contrast to the fading blaze at the festival, is both permanent (it prevents his followers from ever again 'walking in darkness') and universal (it reaches into all 'the world'). However, as this Gospel indicates at the beginning, the light 'shines in the darkness',[2] and the dialogues which follow, involving strong controversy, illustrate the extent of that darkness. Jesus' hearers are forever asking what he really means (v 22) and who he thinks he is (v 25), so it is no surprise when we are told, 'They did not understand...' (v 27).

In approaching these readings we must keep in mind the great claim of the opening verse. The 'headline' text here is that Christ is 'the light of the world' (v 12). If there are hard sayings in these chapters, their purpose is to bring light where there is darkness. That applies not just to the original hearers and readers, but to us as well: our first priority must be to ensure that we follow him who is the true source of light in the darkness of our world.

Are we in danger of underestimating the darkness of the world, and therefore the light of Christ? Pray for grace to follow Jesus today, and claim the promise of verse 12.

[1] Exod 13:21 [2] John 1:5

PERILS OF A NOMINAL FAITH

Jesus warns nominal believers that only by 'holding' to his teaching can they become real disciples. Think about what it means to hold on to the teaching of Christ.

JOHN 8:31–47

The people addressed in this passage belong to a distinct group and had initially felt attracted to Christ since, John tells us, they had 'believed him' (v 31). They are probably to be identified with the group who had 'put their faith in him' (8:30). In speaking to these nominal believers, Jesus stresses the need to hold to his teaching in order that they should really be his disciples.

The subsequent dialogue reveals the utter inadequacy of a merely intellectual knowledge of Christ. Surface-level faith can exist without the deeper levels of the human person, involving submission (v 31), full liberation (v 36), and love (v 42), ever being opened up to Jesus. Christ's intention remains one of grace and mercy, so that his searching exposure of what is really going on in the hearts of his religious enemies is intended to shake their arrogance and pride and bring them to the recognition of who he really is.

Just before this note was written I heard a previously unknown interview with John Lennon, in which he declared his 'belief' in Jesus. He added that he also believed in Muhammad, Buddha, and whatever other gods there might be. Jesus' words here warn us that such surface-level 'admiration' for him will not do; indeed, it can be positively lethal! If he really is the 'light of the world' then nothing less than full surrender to him will do, combined with a commitment to allow him to be our teacher and guide in a life characterised by truth and freedom. 'There is nothing in God's universe that is so utterly useless as a merely formal Christian … [He] knows enough about Christianity to spoil the world for him, but he does not know enough about it for it to be of any positive value.'[1]

Look again at the contrast between the people described in 8:30,31, and pray for the faith that results in real discipleship.

[1] DM Lloyd-Jones, 1899–1981, physician, preacher and author

GOOD SAMARITAN INDEED!

Open our eyes, Lord, we want to see Jesus. Deliver us from the blindness, or even partial sight, which so misled his enemies, and let us recognise Christ's true glory.

JOHN 8:48–59

In this passage the controversy between Jesus and his religious opponents reaches its climax. People who had 'believed him'[1] now repeatedly accuse him of being demon-possessed and end by picking up stones with which to kill him (v 59)! This act of rejection was prompted by the claim of Jesus to have existed before Abraham and by his use of the phrase 'I am', with its unmistakable echo of the divine name revealed in Exodus 3:14.[2]

Christ's claim to be the revelation of the very being of God is not simply a matter of words, not just a theological issue. His opponents not only ascribe his words and deeds to the power of the devil, they also suggest that he is a 'Samaritan' (v 48). This is a term of extreme abuse, reflecting the hatred felt by strict Jews for this despised people – a religious and ethnic division on which John has commented elsewhere.[3] In this way Jesus is disowned as someone whose entire way of life suggests to his enemies that he does not belong among them.

Recall for a moment Jesus' parable of the good Samaritan.[4] This wonderful story depicts a hated 'outsider' who reveals by his actions a love for a suffering human being. It was a scandal that Christ should depict a Samaritan displaying compassion and mercy, demonstrating that he knew the living God, when these very attributes were absent in the lives of those who boasted of their orthodoxy. When Jesus' enemies abused him as a 'Samaritan', they spoke more truth than they realised. In his life of perfect love, the 'good Samaritan' ceased being a fiction and became flesh and blood! This is what God is like – and, like the Samaritan in the parable, Jesus will now (ch 9) demonstrate God's great love for someone at the margins of society.

Try to find time today to reread the parable of the good Samaritan. What are the implications for your Christian life of Jesus' closing words: 'Go and do likewise'?

[1] John 8:31 [2] The Greek also echoes Isa 43:10–13 [3] John 4:9 [4] Luke 10:25–37

BREAKING WITH TRADITION

When I meet with suffering, Father, whether my own or other people's, thank you that I can learn from Jesus, who can give me wisdom, healing words and deep sensitivity.

The night before this note was written the TV news reported a terrible road accident in which six young people, all under 25 years of age, died in a head-on collision. Local people had begun to place flowers at the scene, bearing heart-wrenching inscriptions expressing sympathy and a desolating sense of confusion. We cannot ignore the reality of human suffering and the problems it presents to faith.

Silence is often the only appropriate response to such situations. Indeed there are some things that we should not say – and this is the lesson Jesus' disciples are taught here. Their question as to whose sin was responsible for the condition of the man blind from birth (v 2) rests upon two assumptions: suffering is always related to human sin, and it is a form of punishment inflicted by God himself. Such views can be illustrated by the rabbinical saying: 'There is no death without sin, and there is no suffering without iniquity.' This was the view of Job's friends in the Old Testament, and it remains widespread today, when people ask: 'What have I done to deserve this?'

Jesus' answer is emphatic: 'Neither this man nor his parents sinned' (v 3). The automatic connection between sin and suffering, as though the one always follows the other as cause-and-effect, is here decisively broken on the authority of the Son of God. Jesus takes it further than this, indicating that in some profound way human tragedy can be caught up in the redemptive work of the God who will be 'making everything new'.[1] Suffering may still leave us speechless, but in the light of Christ some traditional statements concerning it can no longer be excused.

Meditate on these words: 'Praise be to the God and Father of our Lord Jesus Christ, the Father of compassion and the God of all comfort, who comforts us in all our troubles, so that we can comfort those in any trouble with the comfort we ourselves receive from God.'[2]

[1] Rev 21:5 [2] 2 Cor 1:3,4

POWER WITHOUT GLORY

'A person with a testimony will never be at the mercy of someone with an argument.' Lord, I praise you for the importance of faithful testimony in this story.

JOHN 9:13–23

The miraculous healing of the blind man created a tremendous stir, first among his neighbours (vs 8,9) and then among the religious leaders (vs 13-16). So great was the impact that the healing results in an official investigation. The Pharisees summon the man himself, then his parents, and subject them to intimidating questioning. The religious authorities possessed real power. They could put people 'out of the synagogue', resulting in social and economic isolation. This explains the parents' fear (v 22) and their reluctance to support their son's testimony. One might compare this with the fear that parents may have today in certain Muslim countries when one of their children becomes a Christian.

The narrative shows how religious power can be used to defend entrenched beliefs and traditional privileges when they are threatened by evidence demanding radical change. The interrogators use every trick to cow their witnesses: invoking Sabbath law, questioning the man's own biography, and, finally, the threat of punishment. At the centre of the incident, however, is the man's own radiant testimony: 'He is a prophet' (v 17). His knowledge of the identity of Jesus will later grow and deepen, but here he uses the language he already knows to withstand the pressures of those who want him to deny his own experience. Jesus claimed: 'I am the light of the world.'[1] The blind man has seen that light and knows himself both physically healed and spiritually enlightened. He cannot be silenced, bribed or intimidated, because no matter what the cost, he must confess the transformation in his life, and the One who has brought this about. The contrast is stark: the blind are given sight, but those who think they see remain in deepest darkness.

Thank God for people you know who are faithful witnesses, and pray for those who are placed under pressure by people with power.

[1] John 8:12

MAN ON TRIAL: PART TWO

'Blessed are those who are persecuted because of righteousness, for theirs is the kingdom of heaven.'[1] Help me, Lord, to see what this means in today's passage.

JOHN 9:24–34

The investigation now moves to a new stage with the recalling of the star witness for further questioning and the atmosphere changes, both because the interrogators become more threatening and because the healed man is increasingly bold. To the Pharisees' dogmatic opening statement, claiming that Jesus 'is a sinner', the man first states his non-negotiable testimony, then moves on to the offensive! As the trial proceeds, he realises the absurdity of the arguments deployed by his questioners and begins to mock their approach (v 27). He even dares to challenge their theological presuppositions (vs 30–33). This enrages the religious leaders, who resort to abusive language and the exercise of brutal power in throwing him out (v 34).

It is difficult to read John's story without smiling. When power is used in such an oppressive way it becomes absurd and deserves parody and scorn. The Bible speaks of God himself laughing at the foolish claims of mortal men, and when religious leaders are obsessed with their own authority and dignity and blind to the miracles of grace, they deserve mockery – but the humour also arises from the healed man's growing convictions and seeming relish for the debate! For someone who has only recently met Jesus, he grows in knowledge and courage with amazing speed. New converts sometimes put us to shame by their boldness and speed in learning!

The man's accusers yet again say more than they intend when they declare: 'You are this fellow's disciple!' (v 28). Intended as a dismissive insult, this is in fact a badge of honour, recalling Jesus' words, 'If you hold to my teaching, you are really my disciples.'[2] This man has had very little teaching, but he holds to it like a limpet and presents us with a shining model of genuine discipleship.

Being 'thrown out' or excluded from society is costly and painful. Pray for all disciples of Jesus who suffer in this way.

1 Matt 5:10 2 John 8:31

THE SHEPHERD AT WORK

Help me, Lord, to visualise the actions of Jesus that are described here, so that I may see the Good Shepherd at work.

JOHN 9:35–41

This passage contains one of the most beautiful statements in the Bible, as John informs us that Jesus, having heard that the healed man had been thrown out, went and 'found him' (v 35). Could there be a more wonderful illustration of the claim that Christ will soon make to be the 'good shepherd'?[1] We must allow our hearts, our imaginations, to work on this statement for a while: to try to visualise the Son of God scouring the lanes and alleys of Jerusalem in search of this disciple, now 'thrown out' from society and perhaps unable to return home to his bewildered and fearful parents.

When he does 'find him', notice the way Jesus gently leads this new believer, step by step, into a deeper knowledge of himself, until the climax is reached with the statement: 'and he worshipped him' (v 38). We are reminded that faith is a journey. For this man it begins with an experience in which the gift of sight is wondrously granted and proceeds with the confession of the uniqueness of Jesus with whatever language is to hand within the convert's existing vocabulary, before finally arriving at the stage at which the disciple can say, 'Lord, I believe'. At this point, understanding has caught up with experience and the mind begins to get the measure of what the heart already knows!

We must keep a life-transforming encounter with Jesus as foundational to the life of faith and recognise that new disciples must be allowed time to grow in the knowledge of the One who has opened their eyes. To reverse this and demand an understanding of systematic theology as a condition of faith is to turn the good news upside down and put a burdensome cart before the gospel horse!

This passage requires imaginative reading. Let your imagination feed on what the phrase 'when he found him' implies – for the blind man, for yourself and for others for whom you pray.

[1] John 10:11; *see also* Luke 15:3–7

LIFE IN ALL ITS FULLNESS

I praise you for the wonderful nature of the freedom I have in Christ, Father; please enable me to live life to the full as I follow him.

JOHN 10:1–10

In the Old Testament the kings of Israel were often described as 'shepherds'. This language reflected Israel's experience as a pastoral people, seen in the humble origins of King David who was called from shepherding sheep to become the 'shepherd of Israel'. However, the prophetic texts often condemn the kings for abandoning God's flock. Ezekiel accuses them of ruling 'harshly and brutally' and promises the coming of 'one shepherd' who will 'tend them' with justice and compassion.[1]

This prophecy is echoed in John 10, where the claims of Jesus signal his fulfilment of Ezekiel's promises. As the true Shepherd of God's people, Jesus brings an end to the tragic experience of selfish, brutal leadership, and promises that those who follow him will know 'life ... to the full' (v 10). Older versions of the Bible translated this as having life 'abundantly', and this word catches something of Jesus' meaning. Following Christ should never result in a diminution of life but rather leads to its enhancement. Jesus releases people from exploitation and bondage and sets us free to live a truly human life.[2]

However, the gift of 'life to the full' has a political and economic dimension. Ezekiel promised that the coming King would 'shepherd the flock with justice'[3] and we must avoid spiritualising the promise of Christ in a way that eclipses this dimension. The new life Jesus promises is more than material blessing, but it includes social transformation. His challenge to the Pharisees was that the burdens they placed on Israel, and especially on the poor, demonstrated that they belonged in the line of false shepherds condemned by the prophets. Jesus, by contrast, brings a new type of rule, a new politics that will deliver those whose lives are being crushed and destroyed, freeing them to live life 'to the full'.

'There is nothing cramping or restricting about life for those who enter his fold.'[4] Is that true to your experience of Christianity and the Church?

[1] Ezek 34:23 [2] Gal 5:1 [3] Ezek 34:16 [4] Morris, *John*, p509

THE OTHER SHEEP

Help me, Father, to share Jesus' vision for the sheep beyond the 'fold' and show me how I might make the good news known there.

JOHN 10:11–21

The controversy recorded here will eventually lead to Jesus' death, and John tells us that his opponents again picked up stones to kill him (v 31). In this atmosphere it is not surprising that we hear Christ reflecting on his impending death.

Jesus asserts that his death will be an act of love for the sheep of his fold, intended to protect them from evil and to secure the promised new life (v 11). Then the horizon broadens out and it becomes clear that the sacrifice the Good Shepherd will make has much wider significance and will bring deliverance and life to 'other sheep' who are at present beyond the range of the Shepherd's voice (v 16). Suddenly we are reminded that the conflict taking place here, which could seem a local affair, has global, even universal, implications. At the start of this Gospel, John the Baptist is heard declaring that Christ is the Lamb of God who 'takes away the sin of the world',[1] and Jesus now anticipates that as the outcome of his sufferings and death.

The love of Christ for 'other sheep', and his determination that he 'must bring them also' into the 'one flock' (v 16) is a rebuke to the parochialism and exclusiveness that has so often characterised the Cchurch. If the death of the Good Shepherd has a global significance, it is scandalous that it has so often been treated as the exclusive possession of the church. Later in the New Testament we hear John insisting that the death of Christ, while atoning for 'our sins', is also 'for the sins of the whole world'.[2] Must we not ask how we can present the good news in ways that will demonstrate the power and relevance of the cross beyond the walls of the church, so that those 'other sheep' may hear the Shepherd's voice and discover the fullness of life that comes through his death?

Who would you identify as being 'other sheep that are not of this sheepfold' today? And what might you need to do to enable them to hear the Shepherd's voice?

[1] John 1:29 [2] 1 John 2:2

SEEING CHRIST – AND GOD

Majesty, worship his majesty; unto Jesus be glory, honour and praise.[1]

JOHN 10:22–30

Some years ago I heard a preacher who had devoted his life to the pastoral care of people on a deprived and violent housing estate. He had suffered much abuse and had been violently assaulted a number of times, yet such was his love for people at the margins of society that he stuck at his task with extraordinary dedication and courage. His sermon remains fresh in my memory when many others, far more eloquent, have long since been forgotten. One thing he said stands out across the years: 'The face of God has been revealed to us in Jesus Christ and, wonder of wonders, it turns out to be a tear-stained face!'

That revelatory comment came to mind when I read Jesus' words at the end of our passage: 'I and the Father are one' (v 30). His claim sparked controversy then (see v 33), and this text also became a theological battleground during later discussions about the doctrine of the Holy Trinity. That Jesus claimed an identity with God the Father seems clear from the fact that he did not refuse the worship of the man to whom sight was restored,[2] and that he later says explicitly, 'Anyone who has seen me has seen the Father.'[3]

However, amid all the necessary and important discussions concerning Trinitarian theology and Christology, we should not overlook what my preacher friend so wonderfully recognised, that if Jesus and the Father are one, not only must Christ be worshipped, but our understanding of God is transformed. Perhaps the anger of Jesus' enemies was kindled not just by what they regarded as blasphemy, but also by the challenge his teaching implied to their understanding of the nature of God. As Joachim Jeremias has said, Jesus teaches that God loves 'the despairing, and for the broken heart his mercy is boundless. That is what God is like, and that is how he is now acting through me.'[4]

Reread verse 30 and let your imagination loose on this text. What does this revolutionary statement really mean for our understanding of God?

[1] Jack W Hayford ©1980 Rocksmith Music [2] John 9:38 [3] John 14:9
[4] J Jeremias, *The Parables of Jesus*, SCM Press, 1972, p144

WHO ARE YOU?

'Who, being in very nature God, did not consider equality with God something to be used to his own advantage; rather, he made himself nothing ... being made in human likeness.'[1]

JOHN 10:31– 42

'How dare you speak to me like that?' we rage inwardly in the face of rude, ignorant or patronising behaviour. Jesus - King of kings - reacts with calm restraint and yet another question for his critics. If they had been willing, it could have led them further in their search for truth.

There's a sharp irony here which prompts our worship. The Jews' accusation is that Jesus 'a mere man, claim[s] to be God'. Of course, the true wonder is that Jesus, who is God, was willing to become man for our sake.[2] Jesus points to his miracles. Do these not indicate his identity? The ordinary people got it: 'Can a demon open the eyes of the blind?' (v 21), and later in this passage we see that 'many believed' (v 42). But the Jewish leaders weren't questioning the miracles: it was their obsession with the letter of the law which led to the charge of blasphemy (v 33) and their desire to kill him (without due process of the Law). So Jesus starts where they are: with the 'Law' or Old Testament. He refers to an intriguing verse in Psalm 82: 'You are "gods"; you are all sons of the Most High.'[3] Various interpretations have been suggested for these words, but whichever we follow, the point is that Jesus could legitimately appropriate to himself the name of 'god' (vs 35,36).

However, it is not time for the final showdown yet. Evading further confrontation, Jesus goes to the place where John the Baptist had given his early witness. Interestingly, John had performed no miracles (v 41); it was his words alone that pointed others to Jesus. They saw what Jesus did and so believed what John had said was true (v 42).

What is it that convinces us that Jesus is God's Son? Allow your questions about Jesus to bring you closer to him – as you search for and listen to his answers.

[1] Phil 2:6,7 [2] DA Carson, *The Gospel according to John*, Eerdmans,1991, p396
[3] Ps 82:6

QUESTIONS

'These [signs] are written that you may believe that Jesus is the Messiah, the Son of God, and that by believing you may have life in his name.'[1]

JOHN 11:1–16

Why does God allow these things to happen? A friend dies unexpectedly; there's yet another disaster; there is so much suffering in the world. Why doesn't God do something? We answer the questions of others, but perhaps, though unexpressed, we have our own nagging doubts. In today's account of the illness of Lazarus we see that the disciples were also perplexed. Even so, courageously, they stick by Jesus. Was Jesus' response to the news of his friend's illness callous (vs 4,6)? Why the apparent delay? Bethany may well have been two days' journey away. With the journey time for the messengers, and then for Jesus and his disciples, Lazarus would have been dead before Jesus' arrival anyway (v 17).[2] Wouldn't it have been easy for Jesus to heal Lazarus from where he was? He had left Jerusalem to escape persecution.[3] It seemed crazy to return to Judea where death might await him – as indeed it did (v 8). Yet, for the sake of his friends, Jesus sets out to Bethany. Thomas, known to us as 'doubting', takes a brave lead (v 16), willing to accompany Jesus whatever his doubts – not understanding, but trusting his Lord.

So, why did Jesus act as he did? Whether historical (as some have questioned) or largely a construct of John, this incident is included purposively in John's Gospel: 'that you may believe' (v 15). This seventh 'sign' demonstrates his omniscience – and his love for his friends and disciples. The purpose is expressed clearly in verse 4. This will not result in death, but… Jesus' words point beyond Lazarus to his own glorification. With hindsight, this miracle, witnessed by his followers, would help them believe in the risen Jesus. As Thomas later responded, so may it prompt our own response: 'My Lord and my God!'[4]

Lord, there are many things about Jesus that we do not understand. Help us to grow in our faith and worship you – our God.

[1] John 20:31 [2] Morris, *John*, p539 [3] John 10:39,40; B Witherington, *John's Wisdom*, Lutterworth, 1995, p202 [4] John 20:28

EXTRAORDINARY FAITH

'I do believe; help me overcome my unbelief.'

JOHN 11:17–27

In the depths of grief, God can seem far away. When Jesus eventually turns up at Bethany it's too late. 'If only you'd been here...', Martha greets Jesus, expressing her sorrow and regret (v 21). The 'in the tomb four days' is significant (v 17). Jews believed that the dead person's soul stayed close to the body for three days, but after that decomposition would have set in.[2] Lazarus is definitely dead.

Martha is sometimes seen as the less 'spiritual' of the two sisters,[3] but here we see her extraordinary faith. We can almost feel her mental anguish as she struggles to make sense of it all. She doesn't understand but, hoping against hope, trusts in Jesus. He accepts what Martha can offer, gently leading her on in understanding and faith – and it brings one of the most momentous 'I am' sayings of Jesus, and one of the Gospels' great confessions of Christ (vs 25,27).

Were Jesus' words in verse 23 just the platitudes of a well-meaning friend? Perhaps Martha thought so at first. All good Jews believed in the final resurrection (v 24). Jesus' electrifying response to Martha's conventional belief must have been shocking. Martha could not have imagined what was about to happen, but she knew she had met the Lord of life, the Messiah, God's Son. 'I am the resurrection and the life', says Jesus. Like Martha, we cannot yet understand the full significance of this redeeming, costly, triumphant proclamation. Yet, in the midst of our own darkness and incomprehension, we too can cling to Jesus – who promises life to all who believe. Like Martha returning from her encounter with Jesus to her household responsibilities, we too are enabled to live our lives as, in the midst of our suffering and questions, we are sustained by faith in our Lord.

Let's bring to God our own suffering, seeking his enabling to trust in him and proclaim with Job: 'I know that my redeemer lives.'[4]

---

[1] Mark 9:24 [2] *See* Witherington, *John's Wisdom*; Morris, *John* [3] Luke 10:38–42 [4] Job 19:25

...AND ORDINARY UNBELIEF

'It is for God's glory so that God's Son may be glorified through it.'[1]

JOHN 11:28-44

Often when we ask God for something, the focus is on us. Yes, we are dependent on God's love for us, but our prayers are centred on our needs and desires. Here we see Jesus, acting out of love for Martha, Mary and Lazarus, but the goal is the 'glory of God' (v 40).

Like her sister, the more emotional Mary expresses her regret over Jesus' too-long absence (v 32). As with Martha, while there is no expectation of the coming miracle, she nevertheless believes that Jesus is capable of supernatural healing. The mourners also lack understanding of Jesus (v 37). Even Martha still hasn't fully understood that they were in the presence of the One who is 'the resurrection and the life' (vs 25,39). The wailing of the mourners and the distress of Mary prompt a notable response in Jesus. The 'deeply moved' of verses 33 and 38 describes not sentimental emotion or ordinary human grief, but indignation, possibly even anger. The bystanders misunderstand his tears (v 36). The word for 'wept' here is the same as that used when Jesus wept over Jerusalem.[2] His sorrow then was in response to the unbelief of the Jews. Commentators suggest that, similarly, Jesus' tears here may be because of the unbelief of those around him (vs 37,39); or, as he stood before the tomb, perhaps it was anger against death – soon to be vanquished.[3]

This seventh sign, like the others in John's Gospel, points to the deity of Jesus. Amid the hubbub of the moment, Jesus never lost sight of his Father's plan (vs 41,42). This astounding miracle points to the climax of Jesus' work on earth, anticipating his own victory over death. His disciples did not understand immediately, but later it would begin to make sense and result in belief that would encompass the world.

Teach us, Lord, to look further than our own needs and to see that your purposes and plans are beyond what we can hope or imagine.[4]

[1] John 11:4 [2] Luke 19:41 [3] 1 Cor 15:54 [4] Eph 3:20

IN GOD'S TIME

'I wait for the Lᴏʀᴅ, my whole being waits, and in his word I put my hope.'[1] Resist the urge for haste, as you listen to God's Word.

JOHN 11:45–57

Do we sometimes miss the true significance of events because we are preoccupied with our own concerns? The resurrection of Lazarus was the catalyst for events that would propel Jesus towards his own death - and glory. Many Jews put their faith in him (was he the Messiah?), but for the unbelieving Jewish leaders this latest miracle was the last straw. They call a meeting. The agenda is Jesus. The action point is summed up by Caiaphas (v 50).

Ironically, the words of Caiaphas sound, with hindsight, as though he truly understood the mission of Jesus - but his plotting is blind to the true purposes of God. What concerns the priests and Pharisees is their own position and power. They aren't disputing the 'miraculous signs' or that many people are believing in Jesus. (Didn't they ask 'Why?'!) Their fear is that with growing popular acclaim for this charismatic leader, the Romans would take action against the potential threat - and their own powerful position in Jewish society would be lost. The solution is brutal: a plot to kill Jesus (v 53). The words of Caiaphas have significance beyond his understanding: Jesus would indeed die for 'the nation', but the Jewish leaders' self-interested plotting would not be rewarded. Their position, their 'temple' and their nation would, in any case, be destroyed in a few years' time (ᴀᴅ 70). Now, as Passover approaches, the story moves irresistibly towards its climax. So, why did Jesus withdraw to a place a few miles from Jerusalem? Maybe it was because he was a wanted man (vs 54,57). Maybe it was because he needed quiet time with his disciples to prepare for the terrible events of the coming week. Or, maybe it was because Jesus - focused on his Father's timing - knew he was to be the Passover lamb.

'For Christ, our Passover lamb, has been sacrificed.'[2] Praise the Lord Jesus that he waited for God's right time – for our sake, for his Father's glory.

1 Ps 130:5   2 1 Cor 5:7

EXTRAVAGANT FAITH

'Though he was rich, yet for your sake he became poor, so that you through his poverty might become rich.'[1]

JOHN 12:1–11

Meals and celebrations were very important in Jesus' life. His ministry began with a wedding feast,[2] and his last act before his arrest was supper with his disciples.[3] Now, as Passover approaches, his friends in Bethany give a meal in his honour (v 2), unwittingly marking the end of his ministry. Lazarus, Mary and Martha could not have known what was ahead. They were caught up in events with a much greater significance than was obvious. This meal, which they intended as a celebration, was turning into a wake.

Exactly one week later, Jesus' body would be lying in a tomb. Unaware of what was to come, Mary carries out an act of unthinkable extravagance (v 3). It wasn't just that the perfume would have cost the equivalent of an average annual salary. The way in which she acted was extravagant too. Having poured the perfume on Jesus, she risked her reputation by unbinding her hair and wiping his feet. How often does our concern about our reputation stop us from offering God what he deserves? Judas' apparent concern for the poor was hollow (v 6), and Jesus moved the focus onto his coming death (v 7). Sadly, his comment about the poor always being with us is used even today as an excuse for individuals and nations to avoid their responsibilities.

Ironically, even though Lazarus had been raised from the dead by Jesus, his identification with Jesus meant that he was again at risk of death (v 10). Followers of Jesus have always had to face the possibility of dying for their faith. The first child converted through Scripture Union's ministry in 1867 was martyred in China in 1900, and I hear today of a Christian charity worker who has been killed in Afghanistan because of her religion. Christian celebrations always have the potential to become wakes.

What for you is the most costly thing about being a Christian?

[1] 2 Cor 8:9 [2] John 2 [3] John 13

FACING THE CROWDS

'Ride on! ride on in majesty! / In lowly pomp ride on to die; / O Christ, thy triumphs now begin / o'er captive death and conquered sin.'[1]

JOHN 12:12–19

Palm Sunday is a great part of our Easter celebrations. Crowds, shouts of acclaim and waving palms lead to exciting praise. But the real event was no piece of street theatre. Like the meal in Bethany, it was a precursor to Jesus' coming passion. For Jesus himself, coming to Jerusalem was full of emotion,[2] and with perhaps two and a half million people there for Passover[3] no wonder the Pharisees were concerned (v 19). As for palm branches, they were not just handy flags for waving, they were a national symbol. And their shouts of praise added something to the psalm they quoted.[4] So what exactly did they mean by 'the king of Israel' (v 13)?

What an opportunity for Jesus finally to take his rightful place, to receive the recognition he deserved! And what did he do? He rode a donkey into Jerusalem. He too was referring back to Scripture (v 15). For those who could understand, this was an important signal. The king of Zechariah 9 was a king who came in peace, but also a king who came for the whole world.[5] In the light of that, perhaps nothing could have been more inappropriate than the crowd's nationalistic palm branches. Today we can be too quick to claim Jesus for ourselves. What exactly do we mean when we talk about a 'Christian country'? Like the disciples, we can be slow to understand (v 16).

In fact there were two crowds that day. Those who had seen Lazarus rise were spreading the word about Jesus (v 17). Their enthusiasm was not just that of popular sentiment – they had witnessed one of Jesus' signs. Their experience of the reality of Jesus' power – like our experience today – was what would ultimately lead to the Pharisees being proved right: 'The whole world has gone after him!' (v 19).

How does the idea of a king who came in peace for the whole world challenge the way you see events in today's news?

---

[1] HH Milman, 1791–1868 [2] Luke 19:41–44 [3] Josephus, quoted by B Milne, *The Message of John*, BST; IVP, 1993, p180 [4] Ps 118:25,26 [5] Zech 9:9

THE UNFINISHED STORY

'For it is in giving that we receive; it is in pardoning that we are pardoned; and it is in dying that we are born to eternal life.'[1]

JOHN 12:20–26

What an extraordinary passage! Jesus is approached by some Greeks – illustrating the concern of the Pharisees in yesterday's passage (v 19). According to Josephus,[2] their presence would not have been unusual since Greek-speaking god-fearers liked to visit Jerusalem at Passover. Yet John tells us almost nothing about them. They speak to Philip, possibly because he had a Greek name (there is a tradition that Philip became a missionary to Gentiles and died near Ephesus[3]). Philip – again with no explanation as to why he didn't go directly to Jesus – tells Andrew. They both tell Jesus (v 22), and that is the last we hear of these Greeks. And yet this passage becomes a hinge for the whole of John's Gospel.

Until now, the hour has always been 'not yet' (2:4; 7:30; 8:20). Suddenly, Jesus' response to the Greeks' request is, 'The hour has come' (v 23). Bruce Milne describes their request to speak with him as triggering 'an exploding fuse in the mind of Jesus'.[4] Now is the time for him to be glorified – but this will not happen through a sophisticated intellectual argument with these Greeks, or for that matter the Jews. Relying on intellectual argument alone is as big a temptation as it has ever been, but, as Paul would later reinforce, at the heart of Jesus' mission is his death on the cross.[5] For the kingdom to grow, the seed has to die (v 24). For many that is still the stumbling block.

There is another turning point here: his followers are drawn into his mission. They face the choice between loving and hating their own lives (v 25). Serving him involves following him to where he goes (v 26). But what a reward! They (we?) will be with him, and honoured by the Father. We are not just onlookers, we are full participants.[6]

Thank God for allowing you to play your part in the unfinished story.

[1] Prayer of St Francis [2] Witherington, *John's Wisdom*, p223 [3] Witherington, *John's Wisdom*, p223 [4] Milne, *John* [5] 1 Cor 1:22,23 [6] 2 Cor 5:20

THINKING AND FEELING

Think of a Christian you know from another country. Thank God that Jesus has drawn his followers from all over the world.

JOHN 12:27–36

Many Christians equate the rightness of an action or a decision with how well things went. 'It all happened so smoothly – it must have been right.' Just as common is the fear that difficulties indicate that we have made a wrong decision. So there is something heartening for us here in Jesus' frank description of his feelings at this time of crisis. His heart may well be troubled, but that's no basis for thinking that he has got it all wrong (v 27). Right through his life he had known that he was born to die, yet he is still troubled by the prospect. Thinking and feeling are inextricably linked. We are not just minds; nor are we just hearts. Recognising that God has made us with differing personalities, how can we keep these two dimensions of our lives in balance?

An interesting aspect of this passage is the interplay between Jesus' private thoughts and his public pronouncements. He moves from the clear conversation with his disciples (vs 23–26) to a statement which turns into a prayer to the Father (v 27). This in turn shifts into a conversation with the crowd. Far from being a sign of confusion or mental stress, is this a model for our own prayer life, an ongoing conversation between us, those around us and our Father?

At this moment, a voice from heaven is heard – the only time in this Gospel. The Father replies to Jesus' request (v 28). Most people fail to hear it. For some it is 'just' thunder. Others think that an angel has spoken to him, even though God had spoken for their benefit (v 30). As Jesus often said, to hear the voice of God we need to be active listeners.[1] No wonder it was so hard for them to grasp what lay ahead for him (vs 31–34).

How can you develop your active listening to God today?

---

[1] Mark 4:9,23; Luke 8:8; 14:35

LIGHT FOR THE BLIND

'For God did not send his Son into the world to condemn the world, but to save the world through him.'[1]

'If we saw these healings and miracles in our church,' someone once said to me, 'then people would believe and we'd see people becoming Christians.' If only that were true. Even when Jesus did miracles on earth, many people didn't believe (v 37). That's not to say that we shouldn't pray and ask for God to work in powerful ways, but if we see that as the sure way to win people to Christ we're li kely to be disappointed – the history of the church is overflowing with examples.

Unbelief and spiritual blindness are powerful forces that we ignore at our peril.[2] At one time there was a fashion for evangelistic surveys that led people through a series of questions. At the end there was only one logical response, which was for respondents to say that they wanted to become a Christian. But life is not as simple as that. Christian faith is not just about intellectual understanding. It's also about a commitment of the will. So even though some of the Jewish leaders had come to believe in Jesus, their desire to be accepted in their own community stopped them from making a real confession of faith (vs 42,43).

Now John returns to the thread which runs right through this chapter: mission. The reason for Jesus coming into the world is that we might believe, not just in a general 'religious believer' sense but believing in the one who sent him (vs 44,45). It's easy to lose sight of God's ultimate purpose. We might not understand God's ways (eg v 40) but we can be sure of what he desires for each one of us: that we will be saved (v 47). What John had said so clearly in one of the best-known parts of his Gospel[3] he now sources to Jesus himself (vs 46-48).

'They loved human glory more than the glory of God' (v 43). Is this a danger for you?

[1] John 3:17 [2] 2 Cor 4:4 [3] John 3:16–21

SHOWING LOVE

For meditation: 'Our Father in heaven…' As you face the challenges of a new day, come to God and be glad that you are his child.

JOHN 13:1–17

Feet become dirty on the dusty roads of Palestine and a good host would normally provide water for his guests to wash before dinner, but he would not normally wash their feet himself, and Jesus did not normally do this either. This was an exceptional act for a solemn moment. Jesus is about to leave the disciples and go to the cross, and before he does so John explains that 'he now showed them the full extent of his love' (v 1, NIV).

How then did Jesus show his love for us? First, he laid aside his glory. Notice how John slows the action down (vs 3–5) so that every detail recalls the much greater self-emptying involved in his becoming flesh and coming into the world.[1] Second, he burdened himself with our sins. Washing is a substitutionary business! You start with clean water and dirty feet and end up with clean feet and a bowl of dirty water (and your own clothes may become wet and soiled). In the same way on the cross, 'God made him who had no sin to be sin for us, so that in him we might become the righteousness of God.'[2]

Love always seeks a response. How then may we respond to his love and show our love for him? First, we must receive his love for ourselves. In the story we see Peter struggling with this (vs 6–9). Beware of pride that sounds ever so humble! Second, we must share it with others. No doubt there are many ways in which we need to 'wash one another's feet' (v 14), but since Jesus showed his love in dying that we might be forgiven, it follows that one important way is to forgive one another as God in Christ forgave us.[3]

Brother, sister, let me serve you, let me be as Christ to you; pray that I may have the grace to let you be my servant too.[4]

---

[1] Phil 2:6–8 [2] 2 Cor 5:21 [3] Eph 4:32 [4] Richard Gillard, *Baptist Praise and Worship*, 473

A GOOD MAN CORRUPTED

For meditation: 'Hallowed be your name...' God's names reveal his power and his love. Recall some names now.

Jesus was accustomed to recognising the activity of Satan in anyone and anything that would deflect him from God's purpose.[1] When we read that Judas' betrayal was prompted by Satan[2] and that Satan entered into him (v 27) we should probably not think of demon possession but rather that Judas succumbed to the great lie that God's kingdom can be advanced by force of arms rather than by the power of self-sacrificing love. Judas' reasoning is not recorded, but it is possible that he went out with the intention of provoking an armed clash from which a general uprising would follow. If so, it all went horribly wrong. Jesus did not resist arrest. He declined the way of the sword and allowed himself to be crucified instead. Judas' plans failed utterly, but paradoxically it was through his treachery that God's purpose was fulfilled, as Jesus knew it would be (v 19).

It is a solemn thought that Jesus was betrayed by a close friend, someone he had himself chosen, someone whose feet he had just washed, someone with whom he had shared a meal. Judas was not a wicked person. He was treasurer to the group, someone therefore judged to be competent and reliable. And yet...! Was it just the money?[3] It is suggested that he allowed himself to be deceived by the plausible and popular policies of the nationalist party that hoped to recruit Jesus to its standard. It is sadly true that Jesus can still be betrayed by someone who shares his bread and cup, who perhaps holds office in the church. Any one of us can be taken in, whether by the base attraction of money or sex, or because we simply lose confidence in the gospel and give our loyalty to some movement that supposedly offers quicker results. The fact that God's purposes will not ultimately be defeated by our sin does not lessen our guilt.

We need to take seriously Paul's instruction: 'Examine yourselves, and only then eat of the bread and drink of the cup.'[4]

[1] Matt 4:1–11; 16:22,23 [2] John 13:2 [3] John 12:6 [4] 1 Cor 11:28, NRSV

HOW JESUS GLORIFIES GOD

For meditation: 'Your kingdom come, your will be done, on earth as in heaven...' God's reign visible on earth is a vision to cherish and a promise to claim.

JOHN 13:31–38

'Glorify' (occurring five times in verses 31 and 32) is an odd word. Outside religion it is only used in a derogatory sense. Christian songs tend to use it as another word for 'praise', but it really suggests something like 'reveal in all his love and power'. In this story, Judas has just gone to the priests, setting in motion a chain of events that will lead inexorably to the cross, and in the cross – 'now!' – Jesus will be revealed as the full expression of God's love for the world, and God's love will be fully revealed in Jesus. 'Glorified' means that Jesus will be seen to be truly God, and God will be seen to be exactly as he is in Jesus.

That is the secret of those (like us) who have come to believe in him. So far as the world is concerned, Jesus will no longer be visible, his cross will be ancient history and his resurrection an improbable tale. If the world is ever to believe, then God will have to be glorified again and again in the love that Jesus' disciples show to one another. The task of glorifying God, that is, of revealing his love, is delegated by Jesus to every believer. Each local church is to be a mirror of the love of God which it has come to know in Jesus and which it is now to reflect onto the world around (vs 34,35).

It sounds simple, but like Peter we are flawed disciples, unable to love apart from the Holy Spirit, who will not come until Jesus has been glorified.[1] There can be no Christian ethics without the motivating and saving power of the cross. One scholar writes, 'By the power of the Good Shepherd's sacrifice Peter finally became a good shepherd, and followed in his Lord's footsteps.'[2] And so may we.

What would it mean for you to sing or pray, 'In my life, Lord, be glorified today'?[3]

---

[1] John 7:39 [2] GR Beasley-Murray, *John*, WBC 36; Word, p248 [3] Bob Kilpatrick © 1978

IN MY FATHER'S HOUSE

For meditation: 'Give us today our daily bread...' The prayer that turns worry into trustful dependence.

JOHN 14:1–14

The good news according to John is that through Jesus all who believe become children of the living God.[1] At the end of the Gospel, Jesus, having 'gone away' in death, 'comes back' as the risen Lord and declares to Mary Magdalene that his Father is now our Father and that believers are now his brothers and sisters.[2]

This is what is promised to the disciples here in chapter 14. The disciples are troubled, understandably since Jesus is going away and they are going to be left 'minding the shop'. They are not worried about how they will get to heaven but about how they will live on earth in the absence of Jesus. Jesus assures them that because of what he is about to do they will be able to enjoy the same relationship with God while on earth as he himself has enjoyed while on earth. (To learn more about that relationship, read 5:19,20.) As a result, they will be able to do what Jesus has been doing and continue his work. In particular, they will be able to pray with confidence and find that Jesus continues to live and work through their prayers (v 13).

Some scholars see 'My Father's house' (v 2) as a metaphor for that relationship with God that Jesus enjoyed while on earth ('I am in the Father, and ... the Father is in me', v 10), and which is now promised to the disciples ('I am in my Father, and you are in me', v 20), though most[3] take it as a picture of heaven, God's dwelling place. The good news is that there are many rooms in the Father's house – plenty of room for us all! – and it is to this relationship that Jesus is the exclusive way (v 6).

There are responsibilities as well as privileges in being a child of God. There is room, work and strength for all who need it. Talk to your Father about this.

[1] John 1:12,13 [2] John 20:17 [3] eg Beasley-Murray, *John*, pp249,251

ALL THE HELP WE NEED

For meditation: 'Forgive us our sins...' Confession of sin should be neither perfunctory nor morbid. Name your sins and hear God's word of pardon.

JOHN 14:15-31

As we have seen, the disciples are 'troubled' at the thought of Jesus leaving them. How will they cope without him? Jesus assures them that though he is going away in death, he will return in resurrection (v 19) and 'on that day' (v 20) they will discover that Jesus has drawn them into the same relationship with God that he has modelled for them during his earthly life. We are still living in the light of 'that day', and to all of us who love him he promises that Father and Son – God in all his fullness – will make their home with us (v 23). Interestingly, the word Jesus uses for 'home' (*moné*) is the same as the word he used for the many 'rooms' in the Father's house (v 2, NIV). We dwell in him as he dwells in us.

The way in which we experience this indwelling is through the person of the Holy Spirit, called here 'another Counsellor' (v 16, NIV). 'Another' means that he will do for the disciples and for us what Jesus himself had done during his earthly life. As such, his work is twofold: to teach us by reminding us of Jesus' teaching and showing us how it applies in the changed circumstances of our day (v 26), and to enable us to witness by convincing the world of the truth about Jesus.[1] The NIV's choice of 'Counsellor' is an attempt to express both functions, teacher and advocate. He is sent by the Father in the name of Jesus to all who, by faith, have become sons and daughters of God.[2] That is our secret. As the hymn puts it, 'For none can guess its grace, / till he become the place / wherein the Holy Spirit makes his dwelling.'[3]

If we know little of the Holy Spirit's indwelling in experience, as promised to all who obey Jesus' teaching (vs 15,16,21,23), are we neglecting Jesus' new and great commandment (13:34)?

---

[1] John 16:8 [2] Gal 4:6 [3] RF Littledale, 1833–90 (after Bianco da Siena, d1434), 'Come down, O love divine'

JOY TO THE WORLD

For meditation: 'Our Father in heaven...' In your meditation, give value to every word.

Why do people plant vines? The vine is not grown for its strength. It does not provide timber to build ships or construct houses. Instead it provides grapes: grapes that make wine, 'wine that gladdens human hearts.'[1] In Scripture, wine is often found as a symbol of blessing, celebration and joy.[2]

The vine is also a symbol for Israel, God's people, because God called Abraham and his descendants to be the means of the world's healing and the source of its joy.[3] So when Jesus says he is the true vine he is drawing on this imagery to declare that he embodies a renewed people of God, and that in him the ancient purpose of God for his people finds fulfilment, to bring joy to the world. 'You are the branches' (v 5) means that in union with him we are called to the same mission. The vine with its branches is not just a picture of how a person can be happy in Jesus; it is a picture of the whole people of God, and of our calling to bring joy to the world.

Of course we can only do this if we remain in him. This means both putting our trust in him and maintaining that faith through difficult times, and also obeying his commands, especially the command to love one another (vs 9-17). There is a warning here against drifting away in unbelief, or of trying to go it alone in isolation from other Christians. By its very nature, the vine is a symbol of that mutual 'abiding', he in us, we in him and in one another. Bringing joy to the world is something we can only do together, as we 'believe in the name of his Son, Jesus Christ, and ... love one another'.[4] We abide by obeying and we obey by abiding.

How is your local church helping to bring joy to the world, and what part should you be playing in this?

---

[1] Ps 104:15 [2] Gen 27:28; Hos 2:8; Joel 3:18; John 2:1–10 [3] Gen 12:3; Ps 80:8,9; Isa 5:1–7 [4] 1 John 3:23

THE WORLD'S HATRED

For meditation: 'Hallowed be your name...' Where? How?

JOHN 15:18 – 16:4

The vine and its branches is such a peaceful picture of the Christian life, as if we were to spend our days ripening against a sun-drenched wall in a beautiful garden, producing the fruit of Christian character that Paul calls the fruit of the Spirit.[1] Bringing joy to the world sounds a rewarding and even glamorous activity, quite literally a 'plum' job! If that is what the disciples thought, they must have experienced a severe shock when Jesus went on to speak not of the world's joy but of its hatred.

'The world' is prominent in John's Gospel. While it sometimes means the created universe or the totality of human beings,[2] more usually it refers to human society organised in rebellion against God. God loves the world, but the world hates God because it rejects his right to judge and to forgive.[3] For this reason Jesus knows that it will crucify him and persecute his followers. The world is not necessarily irreligious, however. On the contrary, Jesus saw the world operating through intensely religious Jewish leaders, and as I write Christians are being driven from their homes in Iraq and murdered in Orissa by people who think that they are 'offering a service to God' (16:2). In the past, Catholic and Protestant Christians have done the same.

Yet all this is somehow within the saving purpose of God. Jesus did not bring joy to the world in spite of being crucified but because of it, and the church does not bring joy to the world in spite of being weak or persecuted but because of it. The seed must fall into the ground and die if there is to be a great harvest.[4]

Faced with the world's hatred, we may retaliate – with hatred; or we may totally withdraw from the godless world – and become part of it! To which are you most tempted?

[1] Gal 5:22,23   [2] John 1:10   [3] John 3:16,19   [4] John 12:24–26

ADVOCATE AND GUIDE

For meditation: 'Your kingdom come, your will be done on earth as in heaven...' Our hope for the future... and our responsibility in the meantime?

JOHN 16:5–15

Shakespeare famously wrote that all the world's a stage on which men and women are players.[1] For John, all the world's a courtroom in which is being argued out the great lawsuit between God and the world. The suit is brought against God by 'the prince of this world' (v 11), who will argue that God is not faithful to his promises and that God's way of love doesn't work. Appearing for the defence stands Jesus, who is both advocate and witness. By his life and teaching he shows that God is true and that trusting God makes sense.[2] By submitting to a cruel death and being raised to life again, Jesus wins a stunning victory and the prince of this world loses his case.[3]

Despite this defeat, the accuser fights on bringing his case against the followers of Jesus, and now it is we who are called to be witnesses by our words and our lives.[4] God has not left us to carry that burden alone: he has given us the Holy Spirit, who will continue the work of Jesus in each new generation. His task is to bring home to people the meaning of Easter, showing that Jesus has won and that continued unbelief is without justification. Like any counsel, the Advocate must hear all witnesses, and the only witnesses who will serve the case are those who are walking in God's way of love and choosing God's weapons.

Now we see why it is for our good that Jesus goes away (v 7). He goes away to fight the fight and win the victory that only he can win, but he goes so that he may come back to us in a way that enables him to be with us for ever as our Advocate and Guide.

'The Spirit will receive from me what he will make known to you' (v 15). This should also be the ambition of every preacher and the prayer of every congregation.

---

[1] *As You Like It*, II, vii, 139 [2] John 3:32–34 [3] John 12:31; Rev 12:10
[4] John 15:27

A LITTLE WHILE

For meditation: 'Give us today our daily bread…' Talk to God about the work you do and the strength you need.

JOHN 16:16–33

'In a little while you will see me no more, and then after a little while you will see me' (v 16). Jesus is speaking of his death and resurrection. Within a few hours Jesus would be taken from them, arrested, tried and executed. His followers would be plunged into grief, while his enemies would be quietly satisfied that a threat to law and order had been eliminated. But not for long! Within a very short time his followers would see him again, alive and victorious.

What was true for those first disciples is true for all Christians. The cross and resurrection stamp their pattern on all Christian living. We do not now see Jesus. The forces of evil often seem invincible and victorious. In this world, as he said, we have trouble (v 33), but we press on because we know that the decisive victory has already been won by Jesus, and that we shall see him again when we die or when he comes again in glory. The resurrection stamps the words 'a little while' on all life's troubles; they are real enough, indeed, but they are temporary, as both Peter and Paul were to testify.[1]

Our present life in this world is marked by struggle. We experience terrible reverses, as when Christian workers are shot by those who see them as a threat, but because of the victory of Jesus we enjoy a new relationship with God as Father (v 27).[2] Living in the Father's house as his sons and daughters we find it a place of answered prayer and fruitful work (v 23). So the upper room discourse ends where it began,[3] with the troubles of being a disciple in this world met by the assurance of the Father's love.

The words, 'Take heart' (v 33), could simply be translated, 'Courage!'. Who do you know who is in need of courage today? How could you encourage them?

---

[1] 1 Pet 5:10; 2 Cor 4:16–18 [2] *See also* John 1:12,13 [3] John 14:1–14

THE LORD'S PRAYER

For meditation: '... as we forgive those who sin against us.' Well?

The first thing to notice about this passage is that it is a prayer. Throughout chapters 14-16 Jesus has been addressing the disciples, giving them his final instructions before he leaves this world and goes to the Father. This is different. Jesus is no longer telling them what do. Instead, 'Jesus places the church's future in the hands of God and invites the church to listen in on that conversation.'[1]

It is commonly said that Jesus prays first for himself (vs 1-5), then for the disciples (vs 6-19), and then for future generations (vs 20-26). It would be more accurate to say that Jesus prays that God will be glorified, first through himself, then through the church and finally in the world. The first part of his prayer does indeed focus on himself, but he is not asking anything for himself, but that God will be fully revealed in the terrible events that are about to unfold. We may not pray, 'Glorify me', but we can and do pray, 'Glorify your name'.

Then Jesus prays for his church, and the heart of his prayer lies in the words, 'Sanctify them by the truth' (v 17). 'Sanctify' does not mean 'make them pure', it means 'take them for your own and set them to do your work'. 'Holy' means 'set apart for God' before it means 'morally upright', but Jesus knows that the church can so easily be derailed by immorality, pride or faction, so he prays, 'Protect them ... so that they may be one' (v 11). The church's unity is not for itself but for the world's sake, that the world may come to believe in Jesus. As he prays for the church's witness (v 20), he prays for those whom God gives him to join him in the Father's house (v 24).

As you listen in on that holy conversation, how might it change which things you talk to God about and which people you pray for?

---

[1] G O'Day, 'John', *New Interpreter's Bible*, Vol IX, Abingdon, 1993, p797

CHOICES

'You made us for yourself and our hearts find no peace until they rest in you.'[1]

JOHN 18:1–18

The momentum is building up, and played out before us is a series of events that take us step by step towards the culmination of Jesus' ministry on earth in the cross and resurrection. Each step of the way is shaped by the choices that individuals make. Judas chooses to go through with his decision, the motive of which is never really clear, to betray Jesus to those who wanted him out of the way. He guides soldiers and religious officials, complete with weapons, to where he knew Jesus would be.

Jesus chose to identify himself to the soldiers, taking such authority in the situation that they were momentarily overwhelmed. He makes a simple and shocking statement in identifying himself, and in so doing points us to his divine nature as the 'I am' (vs 5,6), the one from all eternity equal with his Father.[2] He took the initiative. He was no victim of circumstances. In fact, he had earlier insisted that he would lay down his life of his own accord, that no one would take it from him.[3]

Annas, regarded by the Jews as high priest for life although he had been succeeded by his son-in-law Caiaphas through Roman appointment, chose once more to ignore all that Jesus was. And Peter makes several choices, all on the spur of the moment. He reacted with violence despite knowing from previous experience that Jesus would only be seized if he permitted it.[4] Peter impetuously follows the armed posse with their captive, and then he panics, choosing, when asked, to deny his relationship with Jesus. We too make daily choices, however small, which contribute to the bigger picture of the direction of our lives. Our choices have consequences. They reflect how seriously we take the teachings of Jesus in shaping our lifestyles and relationships. They demonstrate who is Lord of our lives.

Consider what influences the choices you make about how you live out your faith in private and in public.

[1] Augustine of Hippo, 354–430 [2] Tom Wright, *John for Everyone: Part 2*, chapters 11–21, SPCK, 2002, p103 [3] John 10:17,18 [4] John 7:30,44

WHICH KINGDOM?

Pray the Lord's Prayer slowly a couple of times, then pray about your day, focusing on the phrase, 'May your kingdom come'.

JOHN 18:19–40

At no point does Jesus seem out of control of the situation, even when he's being slapped about the face by an official. He communicates a quiet authority that infuriates and frustrates his captors. This is power of a different order. Pilate would have been familiar with claims of kingship and people seizing their way to the crown through violent revolution. Judas Maccabeus had established his dynasty 200 years earlier through military force against the Syrians. Herod the Great had defeated the eastern empire of the Parthians 30 years before Jesus' birth, following which Rome, in gratitude, allowed him the title of 'King of the Jews'.[1] He therefore treats this unwelcome early morning situation with wily caution, attempting to outdo the Jews in their political manoeuvring and to find out who he really is, this unusual man standing before him.

Jesus' answer to the question about being king of the Jews is both incriminating and deeply revealing. He makes clear that his kingdom does not come from this world, that it is radically different in origin and quality. It is not about violence, political manipulation, power plays and one-upmanship. It's not about controlling people – it's about serving them. He had not come to lead a military revolution, but nor had he come to leave people's lives unchanged. His kingship was about bringing truth, the sort that would set people free.[2]

The quality of this kingdom is demonstrated by Jesus washing his disciples' feet, touching and healing lepers, welcoming the hospitality of despised tax collectors, and counting prostitutes among his friends. He had deeply uncomfortable things to say to religious leaders and yet gave time and attention to those regarded as least important by the society of the day. If we are leaders in some context, which kingdom does our behaviour reflect?

Pray for those with authority that they would exercise it wisely and generously – for the judiciary, local politicians and national government.

[1] Wright, *John for Everyone* [2] John 8:32

USE OF POWER

'Look at this man, and you will see your living, loving, bruised and bleeding God.'[1]

JOHN 19:1–16a

The theme of power and its use and misuse is woven all the way through Jesus' life. Here we see both the religious leaders and the soldiers wrongly exploiting their power, Pilate abdicating from using his power to uphold justice, and Jesus with quiet dignity choosing not to draw on heaven's power to rescue him.[2]

The horror of what Jesus is about to go through is rapidly unfolding. He is rejected by the crowd and in an effort to appease them Pilate arranges for Jesus to be flogged, an experience compounded by further physical and mental abuse from soldiers taking advantage of the situation. Both flogging and striking people in the face were regarded as ways of publicly shaming people.[3] Pilate then dithers about his responsibilities. He had the power to let Jesus go, but the veiled threat about what his Roman bosses would think of him was too much and he acquiesces to the Jews' demands.

The phrase, 'Finally Pilate handed him over to them to be crucified' (v 16a) reverberates down through the centuries to us today. There aren't adequate words for the wrongness of it, the barbarity of the treatment of the God of the universe. It's a breathtaking thought that it was Jesus' love for you and me that placed him there and kept him there. But while we reflect on the riotous glory of that love we also need to see this as a classic abuse of power, and consider the implications of this for situations today where people are victims of similar abuse. What does the wrongness of the treatment of Jesus have to say to us about how power is used in the twenty-first century to perpetrate acts of injustice and violence? Issues include how we treat terrorist suspects, the length of time that people can be imprisoned without trial, and our economic reliance upon the arms trade, which produces weapons to maim and kill others.

Pray for Zimbabwe and other countries in similar situations – and for Western nations to use their power righteously.

[1] Wright, *John for Everyone* [2] See Matt 26:53 [3] Colin G Kruse, *John*, TNTC; IVP, 2003

BELONGING

'See what great love the Father has lavished on us, that we should be called children of God! And that is what we are!'[1]

JOHN 19:16b–30

Jesus' journey to and experience on the cross have been cinematically depicted in graphic, gruesome ways in various films. The trouble is that, by focusing our minds on the horror, these Technicolor presentations can detract from the meaning. Seemingly small details are important – like the fact that the sign Pilate insisted be in place describing Jesus as 'King of the Jews' was written in Aramaic (the local language), Latin (the official language of the Roman empire), and Greek (the almost universal language of educated people). Ironically, this announced to the whole world that Jesus was Israel's Messiah.[2] Equally, the soldiers gambling for Jesus' clothes signposts the big picture of what is happening on the cross in its direct link with verse 18 of Psalm 22 – the psalm from which Jesus' haunting cry of dereliction is also drawn.

However, I want to focus on a poignant scene that takes place before Jesus cries, 'It is finished.' Near the cross is a small cluster of Jesus' family, close women friends,[3] and the disciple John. Jesus' words to his mother and to John, which are only recorded in John's Gospel, carry special significance as a picture of what Jesus' death was to achieve. The fact that Jesus, when he was bearing the weight of all the sin that has ever been and ever will be, takes the time to sort out family arrangements tells us something important! Through Jesus' direct intervention from the cross, Mary and John find a place of belonging and home together, a new relationship of parent and son. On one level this demonstrates his deep love for his mother and friend and the importance he always attached to having time for individuals, but it also points to the new relationship Jesus has made possible for us as much-loved children of our heavenly parent. A new home and a place of belonging for eternity.

Reflect on how your church can become a place of greater belonging for all.

[1] 1 John 3:1 [2] Wright, *John for Everyone* [3] Mark 15:40,41; Luke 23:27,49

PROMISE-KEEPING

'Forbid it, Lord, that I should boast, / save in the death of Christ my God! / All the vain things that charm me most, / I sacrifice them to his blood.'[1]

JOHN 19:31–42

As a church leader I'm often told things in confidence and asked to promise to keep them secret. What then happens is that, while I'm keeping my promise not to share the news (such as that someone is expecting a baby), I find that others have been told and people are wondering why I have not been publicly celebrating the news too! Making and keeping promises are two very different things. We find the latter much harder – but it is not so for God. The striking thing about this chapter of John is the number of occasions (vs 24,28,36,37) that the theme of Scriptures being fulfilled is repeated.

For the disciples, all seemed lost as they were faced with irrefutable evidence of Jesus' death in the blood and water flowing from the spear wound in his side and his body taken for burial. The adventure of being with Jesus was over. Yet we are reminded that in the background are the promises that God has made in the form of prophetic statements about the Messiah, the perfect Lamb of God.[2] There is evidence of the divine hand at work – this was not simply a terrible miscarriage of justice. Jesus had breathed his last following that great cry of completion, 'It is finished!' – a single word in the original language, a word that people would write on a bill after it had been paid.[3] Something had been accomplished, the effects of which would ricochet through time and eternity for evermore.

It is God's faithfulness in honouring the promises he's made that gives room for hope. When all seems desperate and our prayers like dust, then all that is left to us is to trust God, and keep trusting he will keep his promises until the evidence changes. Contrary to all appearances Good Friday was not the end...

Pray for Christians worldwide who are suffering for their faith, for whom times are dark and trusting God is difficult.

---

[1] Isaac Watts, 1674–1748, 'When I survey the wondrous cross' [2] Exod 12:46; Num 9:12; Zech 12:10; see also Rev 1:7 [3] Wright, John for Everyone, Part 2, p131

RECOGNISING JESUS

'Christ behind us in all our yesterdays. Christ with us in our today. Christ before us in all our tomorrows, Alpha and Omega, Christ, Lord of all!'[1]

JOHN 20:1–18

Today's account is full of emotion – turbulent stomach-churning emotion: grief, panic that Jesus' body has been stolen, a desperate adrenalin-pumping dash to the tomb, confusion, glimmerings of hope, and deep distress as the loss of his body sinks in. But we are told that in the midst of this John 'saw and believed' (v 8). In his gut he knew that Jesus had been physically raised from the dead, although he couldn't at that stage make sense of it (v 9).

At that stage Mary Magdalene couldn't see what John saw. Her tears eloquently communicate her confusion and loss. Crying here means 'wailing' as a loud expression of grief. In spite of this, or maybe because of it, the star part is given to her of being first to see the resurrected Jesus. For the newly resurrected Lord to choose to reveal himself to a woman with such a suspect background[2] – this was so 'not politically correct' for that time! Here being worked out is the most stupendous event in all of human history and eternity, and Jesus first stops for a chat with a woman such as Mary. Once again we are struck by the upside-down nature of God's treatment of status and power.

The tender scene of Jesus taking the initiative in addressing her, and then her recognising him as he speaks her name, reminds us that he knows each of us by name.[3] Have you ever felt tossed about by emotion in circumstances outside your control which appear to make little sense? John believed even though he didn't understand, because he recognised that God was doing something. Mary recognised Jesus when he called her by name. The truth is that God is at work in the world around us today, whether we recognise it or not.

Ask God to open your eyes to recognise what he's doing in your workplace or neighbourhood, and give you the courage to join in.

[1] Celtic Daily Prayer, 'Easter Vigil', 2005 [2] Luke 8:2 [3] Isa 43:1; 49:16; Luke 10:20

A NEW BEGINNING

'Storm is the environment in which we either lose our lives or are saved; there is no cool, safe ledge on which to perch as spectators.'[1]

JOHN 20:19–23

What a confusing time for the disciples! A missing body. A first-hand account from a woman, of all people, of having seen and talked with Jesus. John's conviction that Jesus had been raised from the dead when such ideas were considered nonsense by many. Fear that they would be regarded as grave robbers, a capital offence. And then Jesus appears in the room, apparently able to walk through a locked door. This was no ordinary day!

Jesus had told his disciples that they would be scattered and abandon him, and he told Peter that he would deny him. Now, when they were feeling bewildered and deeply ashamed, to hear Jesus speaking peace to them, showing that he wasn't holding their failures against them, heralded a new beginning. He didn't rebuke them for their fear, lack of understanding and disbelief. Rather, he helped them understand that it was really him. He then commissioned them, imparting the Holy Spirit and anticipating Pentecost which was to happen 50 days later.

Jesus' commission, 'As the Father has sent me, I am sending you' (v 21), is significant for us too. Jesus sends out his deeply flawed disciples to be his witnesses. He doesn't wait until we're perfect but works with the grain of who we are, shaping and changing us as we relate to him.[2] John's Gospel speaks often of Jesus being sent into the world: to do his Father's will (6:38,39; 8:29), to speak his words (3:34; 12:49; 17:8), to perform his works (4:34; 5:36; 9:4), and to bring salvation (3:16,17).[3] This is what we too are sent out to do. It is also the manner in which Jesus was sent that is important – 'The Word became flesh and blood and moved into the neighborhood.'[4] We too are called to be with people, empowered and equipped by the Holy Spirit and sharing Jesus in the ways listed above.

Pray about your church's neighbourhood. How could you be more with local people rather than just trying to attract them into church?

[1] E Peterson, *Under the Unpredictable Plant*, Eerdmans, 1994 [2] 2 Cor 3:18
[3] Kruse, *John* [4] John 1:14, *The Message*

DOUBTS AND QUESTIONS

'Blessed are those who have not seen and yet have believed.'[1] Worship God, asking for more revelation concerning God's nature.

JOHN 20:24–31

This story of Jesus' encounter with Thomas has given hope to Christians down through the centuries. Probably a natural sceptic, he comes across as a cautious man who needed to be convinced of something personally before committing himself to it. Earlier references to him show someone determined in his commitment to Jesus and honest about his doubts.[2]

Jesus appears, again coming through a locked door, and engages Thomas immediately and directly. He doesn't dismiss or condemn him for his doubt, but goes to the core of the matter, providing Thomas with the personal opportunity to touch and see. He then instructs him to stop doubting. Thomas' heartfelt response, 'My Lord and my God!' (v 28), is the last of a series of confessions of Jesus recorded in John's Gospel. Others include those of John the Baptist (1:34), Nathanael (1:49), the Samaritans (4:42), the man born blind (9:33–38), Martha (11:27), and the disciples (16:30).[3]

For many Christians the plea of the father of the boy with convulsions – 'I do believe; help me overcome my unbelief'[4] – resonates with their experience. In some churches it is seen as immature or backsliding if one voices searching questions or doubts. We live in an increasingly post-Christian, postmodern, post-most-things age, where everything is up for debate and solid convictions are hard to hang on to. In this context it is vital that we provide space for people to explore their faith and grapple with the hard questions without being judged because they query beliefs we hold dear. God is big enough and generous enough to handle our doubts, as this incident with Thomas demonstrates, and it is by facing them and bringing them to Jesus, echoing the prayer of the boy's father, that we will be able to trust even where we don't understand.

For whom can you provide a safe place to grapple with their questions of faith?

[1] John 20:29 [2] John 11:16; 14:5 [3] Kruse, *John* [4] Mark 9:24

BREAKFAST ON THE BEACH

'Lead us on our journey to places of resurrection; to dwellings of peace;
to healings of wounds; to joys of discovery.'[1]

JOHN 21:1-14

Peter wanted to get on with life, go back to what he knew and could handle - and so the disciples went fishing. However, it didn't go to plan and all their fishermen's knowledge and skills proved fruitless. Again, Jesus comes to them, and again they don't recognise him until history repeats itself and their experience takes them straight back to their first fishing trip with Jesus.[2]

'When they get to shore, what do the disciples find? The risen Lord, master of time and space, who holds the galaxies in place and who knows all people's hearts and will be both judge and the criterion on the last day. And he's sitting there smoking them a few kippers for breakfast.'[3] More than that, although he already has some fish that he's cooking, he asks them for some of theirs and seems to overlook the fact that it was his intervention that enabled them to catch those fish in the first place. He didn't need their fish, but he chose to ask for them anyway.

This is no casual encounter between old friends. It's the third time Jesus appears to his disciples following his resurrection, and there must be a reason for him cooking them breakfast on the beach. This breakfast is about several things. It reinforces their understanding that the resurrection was physical and not just spiritual. It demonstrates our God's involvement in the stuff of everyday life. As the story unfolds we see that it's Peter's opportunity for forgiveness. There's also something here in this story about the relationship between our activities and God's. There's a correction for those of us who err on the side of thinking it's either all down to us or alternatively we should just passively wait for God to act. There's something both humbling and liberating in grasping that he welcomes our contribution but doesn't need it.

As a church leader do you fall into the trap of thinking it's all down to you? If so, remember it's God's church and hand back control to him.

[1] Ray Simpson, *Celtic Daily Light*, Hodder & Stoughton, 1997 [2] Luke 5:4–11
[3] C Gempf, *Mealtime Habits of the Messiah*, Zondervan, 2005

FOLLOWING JESUS

'If we confess our sins, he is faithful and just and will forgive us our sins and purify us from all unrighteousness.'[1] Give thanks for God's grace.

JOHN 21:15–25

Traumatic incidents leave their imprints on our memories. It can be a piece of music, a particular date, or a smell that brings the memories rushing back. And here is Peter on the beach with Jesus with the smell of a charcoal fire in his nostrils, reminiscent of the fire beside which he denied Jesus three times.[2] Drawing Peter to one side, Jesus proceeds to ask him the question that goes to the heart of his guilt and shame: 'Do you love me?' The question is asked and answered three times. Each time of answering, God's grace is at work cancelling out Peter's former denial. Each answer also evoked a challenge to Peter from Jesus, a fresh requirement to exercise responsibility as a shepherd of God's people. He was commanded to provide spiritual nourishment for new believers (lambs) and pastoral care and spiritual nourishment for believers generally (sheep).

This wasn't earning forgiveness or somehow making up for what he'd done. Rather, Peter was being trusted afresh, and that is the nature of grace. 'Not only is this a fresh commission. Not only is Jesus trusting Peter to get back to fruitful work, and to turn his wobbly love for Jesus to good account. It is more: Jesus is sharing his own work, his own ministry, with Peter.'[3] We find Peter later on using similar language in urging church elders to shepherd God's flock.[4] Grace truly received is multiplied as it is passed on to others.

The conversation concludes with Peter being told to concentrate on following Jesus – a simple, uncomplicated but very significant command which is repeated (vs 19,22). God's forgiveness is not merely that we might feel better, although this is often the case. Rather it is so that we can grace others as we continue to follow Jesus. Following him includes expressing a shepherd's love.

'Your feet will bring you where your heart is.'[5] Prayerfully reflect on your direction of travel.

---

[1] 1 John 1:9 [2] John 18:18,25 [3] Wright, *John for Everyone* [4] 1 Pet 5:1–4
[5] Irish proverb (source unknown)

FOR FURTHER STUDY

Here are some other resources from Scripture Union to help you keep on reading the Bible regularly – in your small group and individually:

Whitney Kuniholm, *Essential 100*, Scripture Union, 2010 – a comprehensive overview of the Bible including introductions for different sections, 100 readings with notes, and opportunities to pray and respond. It encourages a holistic head and heart engagement with the Bible alongside intimacy with God.

John Grayston, *Explorer's Guide to the Bible*, Scripture Union, 2008 – for anyone who wants to know more about the Bible but isn't an expert. The book is divided into three main sections to give readers different levels of Bible engagement, ranging from a general overview to a close-up look at each book.

The *God Moments Together* series: small group study material aimed at busy people who are juggling study, work, family, friends, church... These straightforward outlines will help you to meet with God as you get together with others to read the Bible and pray.

The *LifeBuilder* series: small group study material. Many titles including topical and character studies, Old and New Testament books.

THE WRITERS

DR PAUL WOODBRIDGE is
Director of Free Church Ministry
Training and Tutor in New
Testament at Oak Hill College,
North London. He is a football
referee and a keen cricket fan.

FRAN BECKETT OBE is a
consultant in leadership and
governance. She is also leader of
'Restore', an inner-city church-
planting initiative.

DR ELAINE STORKEY is President
of Tearfund, among many other
roles. She has written many books,
including *The Search for Intimacy*
(Hodder & Stoughton, 1995).

JOHN GRAYSTON recently
retired as Director of Theology
for Scripture Union in England
and Wales, and worships at an
independent church in Chelmsford.
He is the writer of *Explorer's Guide
to the Bible* (SU, 2008).

DR CONRAD GEMPF lectures in
New Testament at London School of
Theology. He is the primary author
and presenter of the DVD *Christian
Life and the Bible* (SU).

REV DR STEVE MOTYER works
at London School of Theology
where he leads the Theology and
Counselling degree programme,
and teaches New Testament and
Hermeneutics.

ANNABEL ROBINSON is now
retired. She was formerly Professor
of Classics at the University of
Regina in Canada. She is married
to Reid, with children and
grandchildren in Calgary and in
Oslo, Norway.

RT REV PETER BROADBENT
is Bishop of Willesden. He
was a founder member of the
Archbishops' Council and
convenes the Leadership Team
of Spring Harvest.

PETER KIMBER was Chief
Executive of Scripture Union in
England and Wales. He is now
retired and lives in East Lothian.

THE WRITERS

DR PAULINE HOGGARTH
retired in 2009 from her work as SU's International Bible Minisitries Coordinator. She is currently helping as a volunteer in a church in the city of Armenia, Colombia.

DR IDA GLASER is a Crosslinks
Consultant on Muslim-Christian relations and Academic Director of The Centre for Muslim-Christian Studies, Oxford.

DR DAVID SMITH is Senior
Research Fellow at International Christian College, Glasgow. He has written many books including *Mission After Christendom* (DLT) and *Moving Towards Emmaus* (SPCK).

EMLYN AND 'TRICIA
WILLIAMS Emlyn is Regional Director of SU's Britain and Ireland Regional Council. 'Tricia is Creative Developer (Adults) for SU England and Wales.

REV DR ALASTAIR CAMPBELL
is a Baptist minister. Before his retirement he taught New Testament at Spurgeon's College, London and at the Union Theological College of the West Indies in Kingston, Jamaica.